A TEENAGER'S GUIDE TO A.D.D.

Understanding and Treating Attention Deficit Disorders Through The Teenage Years

Antony J. Amen
Sharon R. Johnson
with Daniel G. Amen, M.D.

Illustrations by Michael Musholt

MindWorks Press   Fairfield, CA

MindWorks Press
350 Chadbourne Road
Fairfield, California 94585
(707) 429-7181

ISBN 1-886554-05-6
Manufactured in the United States of America
9 8 7 6 5 4 3 2 1

Other Books By Dr. Amen

IMAGES INTO THE MIND:
A Radical New Look At Understanding and Changing Behavior
WINDOWS INTO THE A.D.D. MIND
Understanding and Treating Attention Deficit Disorder
(Childhood Through Adulthood)
DON'T SHOOT YOURSELF IN THE FOOT
A Program To End Self-Defeating Behavior Forever
NEW SKILLS FOR FRAZZLED PARENTS
Superior Skills for Parenting Difficult Kids
HEALING THE CHAOS WITHIN
The Interaction Between A.D.D., Alcoholism
and Growing Up In an Alcoholic Home
MINDCOACH FOR KIDS
Teaching Kids and Teens To Think Positive and Feel Good
WOULD YOU GIVE TWO MINUTES A DAY
FOR A LIFETIME OF LOVE
TEN STEPS TO BUILDING VALUES WITHIN CHILDREN
A CHILD'S GUIDE TO A.D.D.
THE SECRETS OF SUCCESSFUL STUDENTS

Confidentiality is essential to psychiatric practice. All case descriptions in this book, therefore, have been altered to preserve the anonymity of patients without distorting the essentials of their stories.

To my family and friends.
Thank you for being there.
AJA

To my mother and father
who have loved me for who
I am and helped show me
who I'm capable of being.
SRJ

To Antony and Sharon, and
the other teenagers with A.D.D.
who have given me the privilege
of being a part of their lives.
DA

Acknowledgments

We would like to thank the many people who have made this book possible, especially our parents who have supported us and helped us to seek professional guidance for the problems we experienced.

Introduction

This book may change your life! No kidding. It may be the difference between finishing high school and going to college, or dropping out and working at fast food places for the rest of your life. Our goal in this book is to help you understand Attention Deficit Disorder (ADD), get the best help for it, and to help you reach your potential, at home, at school, at work and with your friends or sweetheart.

We understand that many teenagers have a problem with getting help, even in the face of obvious problems, such as school failure, drug abuse and fighting with parents. Instead of admitting there are problems they complain that their failures are "not their fault." Common excuses include (we've used these ourselves): "It's the teacher's fault...It's boring...I don't need to know this stuff...My parents expect too much....I'm just stupid....I didn't hear what was said." To get professional help, many teenagers think that they're admitting to being dumb or stupid. Nothing could be further from the truth, because many people with ADD are very bright. They just have a hard time showing it.

For us, getting the right help made all of the difference. Things are not perfect in our lives, but we have finished high school, started college, we both have jobs and we have started to feel good about ourselves for the first time in a long time.

Many people think that ADD is just a fad or something that kids outgrow. Yet, when ADD is left untreated it causes serious life problems. For example:

• 30% of people with ADD never finish high school

• 40% of boys with ADD will be arrested for a felony by the time they're 16

• 52% of people with ADD will have drug or alcohol problems

• 75% of adults with ADD have relationship problems as an adult

Many people think that ADD is just an excuse for poor grades or bad behavior. Teachers and parents often tell kids with ADD that if only they would try harder they'd do better. Unfortunately, that is not true. In fact, the harder people with ADD try, the worse it gets.

ADD is the most common learning problem among children, teens and adults. It affects more than 17 million Americans.

In this book we'll tell you our own stories, to let you know how we struggled and dealt with ADD. We'll tell you what ADD is, how you get it and what to do about it. We'll also get you to think about how you can be more successful at school, at home and with your friends.

This book is based on our own experience of having ADD and on Dr. Amen's experience of treating more than 4,000 children, teenagers and adults with ADD.

Table of Contents

PART I.

WHAT IS ADD?
HOW DO I KNOW IF I HAVE IT?

PART II.

DEALING WITH ADD
DAY-TO-DAY

PART III.
EXCELLING WITH ADD

PART I.

WHAT IS ADD?

HOW DO I KNOW IF I HAVE IT?

Chapter 1:

Our Stories

Sharon (SRJ)

Sharon's Story

Just growing up is hard enough, but having two older brothers and two older sisters doesn't make it any easier. My oldest sister Susan, moved out when I was about three. This is also when my two brothers, Scott and Steve, began to pick on me. They thought it was really funny to hold me upside down by my feet, with my head in the toilet, and flush it. This was called a swirly. I never have found swirlies to be funny. My brothers moved out when I was five, and luckily their fun ended. My parents were left with my older sister, Sarah, and me to deal with.

Competition has always been a serious matter for me; and Sarah was my competition growing up. Unfortunately for me, it always seemed that she was better than me AT EVERYTHING. She had very good grades in school; she usually had a boyfriend (or two); she was prettier than I was; and she liked doing "girlish" things. I struggled in school; I hated even the idea of kissing a boy; I never cared much about what I looked like; and I was the one who'd destroy all of Sarah's girlish toys. We used to fight all the time. Sarah would usually end up crying, and I'd end up in trouble.

When I was four-years-old I started preschool. I thought I was really cool. My teacher told my mom that she thought I needed to exercise somewhere outside of the classroom. Not because I was overweight, but simply because I always had way too much energy. My mom put me into gymnastics.

I started kindergarten at San Mateo Christian Academy. Towards the end of the year, my teacher and my parents decided I wasn't ready to go into first grade yet, so I stayed for another year of kindergarten.

I went to gymnastics three times a week. I also started to play soccer and baseball. I played baseball in an all-boys league. Some of the guys hated the idea of a girl playing. They had this idea that girls weren't good at sports. I loved proving them wrong. My Dad taught me how to play golf the summer before first grade. We played three or four times a month.

I had no real problems with first or second grade, other than the teacher repeatedly telling me to sit still and pay attention. I used to sharpen my pencil two or three times during a class. My teacher bought me a pencil sharpener so that I would stay at my desk.

In third grade I started getting in trouble. I couldn't sit still for five minutes and I had trouble paying attention. Even though I goofed around a lot, I still managed to pull off a B average.

When I was nine, I went to gymnastics four times a week. I was also in my first state competition. I worked hard to learn the routines, and it paid off. I won best All-Around Gymnast at the California State Competition! I also played soccer on a girls traveling team. The age group of the team was thirteen. Most of the girls weren't bothered by me being four years younger.

My first big year of failure came in fourth grade. My grades fell to

D's and F's. I found myself being unable to concentrate in class. Homework became a joke, partially because I didn't pay attention to the directions given in class. I didn't know why I was failing. I tried my hardest, but things only got worse. My mind always wandered. When I was reading it was very hard for me to concentrate on what I was doing. My classmates started to call me stupid and I started to feel stupid. In the fourth grade I started to be the class clown. It made time go by faster and the class thought it was funny.

I started fifth grade telling myself that I wasn't going to fall behind, yet I fell behind the first day when I was supposed to bring papers home and have them signed by my parents. I forgot the papers at school. It wasn't until several weeks later that I managed to get the papers home and back to school signed. The year started off poorly, and it didn't get any better. I started off behind because I missed learning some important things in the fourth grade. The rest of the class was learning how to divide and I couldn't even multiply. I was taken out of sports because my first report card was terrible. I had no idea what I could do to stop failing. After all, I didn't know what I was doing wrong.

I wanted to go to a different school. I wanted to get away from the name calling, failure and hurt feelings. My parents let me go to the public school behind our house.

The change in school didn't help. About a week into the new school I started to have problems. The kids were put into groups of four by the teacher. When it was my turn to be put in a group all of the kids who weren't in my group yelled "Yeah." They were glad I wasn't in their group and I didn't know why. I thought that something must have been written on my forehead saying that I was stupid. It didn't seem that I had a fair chance to change my reputation. I couldn't do much but pretend that the comments and name calling from kids didn't hurt. But because the comments really did hurt, I became hostile and angry a lot.

One day, out of the blue, my parents said we were moving. They also said I could start back at gymnastics. There was only one condition, I had to go to a tutor twice a week.

After a couple weeks back in gymnastics I was asked to preform in a state meet. I was very dedicated. I worked out four times a week, two hours a day. Gymnastics took my mind off my failures. I felt good about myself when I was in the gym. I knew that gymnastics was something I was good at. At the competition, I won first place in all three of my events and also won best All-Around. That same day I was given the opportunity to go to Oregon and train for the Olympics. I said no because I knew I would be concentrating more on gymnastics than school. Education was more important to me.

At the end of the year I hadn't exactly passed fifth grade. I was allowed to go on though. We moved to Danville that summer. I decided I no longer wanted to do gymnastics. So I left my gymnastics ability behind as I moved to my new home.

I started sixth grade in a whole new environment. I met my best friend Christie that year. I think the reason for us still being best friends is because we understand each other. We're both goof balls, and we've both had difficulties in school.

My classes were so big at my new school that hardly anyone got any individual attention. The only kids who received attention from the teachers were the ones who excelled. What about those of us who had a hard time just passing? I thought, no attention is better than negative attention; which is all I would have gotten. I thought there was something about me that let other kids know I was stupid.

Again I struggled in school. Failing at three different schools proved to me that something was wrong.

My parents thought I might have a learning disability, and I hoped I did. They took me to be tested in San Francisco. I only wanted two things from getting tested: to know what was wrong with me and what I could do about it. It took three months of testing and thousands of dollars to have one more person say, "Sharon's just lazy. If she applied herself a little bit more she'd be fine." Both my parents and I knew that I wasn't lazy. I would have done whatever it took for me to be able to learn again. I felt guilty for spending my parents time, energy, and money, to hear that I was lazy.

At the end of sixth grade I continued to fail. The principal said I could go on to seventh grade, but only if I was willing to make up my sixth grade work on my own at the same time. I tried my hardest to accomplish this challenge, but failed. At the end of seventh grade I had not completed either the sixth or seventh grade. I was forced to go to summer school and to a tutor.

For the first time I became rebellious and depressed. I started to smoke marijuana. Getting high helped me to escape the painful reality of failure. I felt my life had no meaning and I had no ambition left. Every time I'd try hard for something that I really wanted it didn't seem to work. It seemed I just set myself up for disappointments (which there were lots of in my life!).

In eighth grade I had to try to make up my sixth and seventh grade work at the same time I was studying eighth grade in order to graduate with my class. My priorities were somewhat screwed up. I'd go to school, come home, get stoned, eat, watch T.V., and then work on my independent homework. My principal told my mom that no one has ever made up sixth AND seventh grade at the same time as passing eighth grade. This gave me a lot of ambition (the competitive part of me started to take over), not only would passing all three grades enable me to go on to high school, but I'd also be the first one who accomplished the task. Even though I was usually stoned, I did it! I was able to graduate with my class! During the summer I saw a tutor twice a week. I didn't go to learn anything new, I went so that I wouldn't forget everything I had learned.

The first day of my freshman year was a complete disaster. I couldn't find any of my classes. By the time I did they were basically over. The second day of school I was already behind. Halfway through the year I was put into resource classes. I felt like I was being treated like some rat in an experiment. My parents then insisted that they test me. Even before they finished the testing the school said I was Dyslexic. Even with resource I failed. I had a grand total of 15 credits for my freshman year (about 25% of what I needed).

My parents and I went looking at boarding schools over the summer. When I wasn't across the country looking at schools I'd go to my new tutor. I didn't have much time for anything, let alone smoking pot. The tutoring center noticed that I had a very short attention span. That was nothing new. My parents noticed that when I was three.

I didn't want to leave my family to go to a boarding school. My mom had heard about a local private school, Spraings Academy. The very first time we looked at Spraings it felt like home. There were 25 students in the school who all had different ways of learning.

I started my sophomore year at Spraings. I still had a very hard time paying attention even with only five students in a classroom. My

English teacher, Mrs. Spencer, knew I was trying my hardest. She was the first teacher who never gave up on me. She made learning easy and fun for me. She also recommended that we go back to the tutoring center that noticed my poor attention span and pursue further testing.

The tutoring center recommended I see Dr. Daniel Amen. The first time we met with Dr. Amen he was sure that I had A.D.D. He put me on Ritalin and he started to see me in psychotherapy. Within the first week of being on medication I completely stopped smoking pot (he told me not to use pot and my medication together because it could cause serious problems). The very first time I took my medication was on a Saturday. It was the first Saturday in 6 years that I spent cleaning my room and organizing my stuff, rather than lounging in front of the T.V.

Learning became easier and fun and my grades actually improved. Things started to get a lot better. I turned 16 and I got my drivers license. My grades seemed to magically turn from F's to all A's and I had no desire to ever try drugs again. Finally, I felt like I was able to make my parents proud of me. School became my major interest. I felt like I had missed a lot of learning over six years of failure. I was determined to make it all up. At the end of the year, my grade point average was 3.9.

My junior year had many obstacles. Ritalin gave me some negative side effects, so Dr. Amen put me on Dexedrine. I also had some problems with depression and getting stuck on certain thoughts so I starting taking Zoloft, an antidepressant medication. Because I was so behind in school I would have had to take two extra years of high school in order to get my high school diploma. Dr. Amen, my parents and I decided it would be a good idea for me to take the California High School Proficiency Examination. If I passed the test I could start at a local junior college under the supervision of the learning disability program.

After I took the test I was positive that I had failed. I had had so many failures that I knew that this would be just another one. I told my family, my friends and even myself that I had failed. Six weeks later the results came to my house. I wasn't even going to open them. I didn't want to see the words, YOU FAILED. My mom took care of that problem. She ripped open the envelope and started to cry tears of joy. I knew then that I had passed. Passing the test proved to me that the support and determination I got from my parents paid off. More importantly, passing the test showed me that I was a reasonably intelligent person and not the stupid idiot the other kids said I was.

I'm now in college and passing my classes. I actually love learning! I'd still be in fourth grade if my parents didn't hold my hand the whole way through and believe in me when I didn't believe in myself. They have only shown love to me through it all. My parents have shown me that I can do anything I want to do. Nothing can get in my way that I can't overcome or work around. In order for me to be successful my ADD needed to be treated. I wish they would have figured it out in fourth grade, but thank God it was discovered so that I can make my life go in the direction I choose. The worst years of my life are in the past, and the best are yet to come!!!

Antony (AJA)

Antony's Story

Until his death when I was 10-years-old, Jim was my biological father. He was tall, good looking and very smart. But he seemed to get himself into lots of trouble. When he was young, his mother told me that he was like three-boys-in-one. He was very active and mischievous. Even though the school said he was an intelligent child, he never performed to his ability. School was boring for him and he had trouble getting his homework done. Jim joined the U. S. Marines when he was 18 years old. He met my mother, Robbin, at a USO dance in Southern California. They dated for nine months and got married when Jim was discharged from the Marines. They moved to Michigan, where Jim's family lived. From what I understand, their marriage was troubled. Jim drank too much and he had trouble keeping jobs. Shortly after I was born in 1977, Jim and Robbin split up and I moved back to Southern California with my mom.

After two years, my mom married Daniel. He was my mom's high school sweetheart. At the time, he was a medical student in Oklahoma, so we lived there for two and a half years while he was in school. During our time in Oklahoma Daniel adopted me, became my day-to-day dad and my name was changed to Antony Amen. He loved me a lot.

When I was little, my mom said I was a handful. She told me about an embarrassing time at the International House of Pancakes Restaurant when I was two-years-old. She went to pay the bill and when her back was turned I climbed a pole and pulled down a vine that was growing up the pole. I spilled the drinks all over the table.

Everyone in the restaurant was staring at my mom and me. When I was three-years-old I went to play outside in the courtyard near our apartment. It was hot outside so I decided to take off all of my clothes, except for my cowboy boots (a boy has to wear his boots!). My mom was talking to a friend when she saw a little boy outside without his clothes on, except for the boots, and she wondered what kind of mom would let her child outside to play without clothes on. She screamed when she found out it was me. At the age of four we got a new puppy. My mom told me not to tease the dog, but I loved to play rough with him. One time I chased the dog under a table and he bit me right in the face. My parents gave the dog away.

After my dad finished medical school he joined the U.S. Army and we moved to the Washington, D.C. area. Dad did his training to become a psychiatrist at Walter Reed Army Medical Center. As an intern, my dad worked long hours and we didn't get to see him much. In the month after we moved, my sister Breanne was born and I started kindergarten. Breanne was a sweet baby and we spent a lot of time together.

Mrs. Beasley was my kindergarten teacher. She told my folks that I was a bright child (like Jim), but I had trouble paying attention (also like Jim). Some of her comments about me were, "He's out in space. He looks around a lot. I have to bring him back to earth." I guess that was why she recommended me for the young astronauts program! When I was in kindergarten I got into many fights with a boy from England, named Charles. When we went to first grade, my mom and Charles' mom made sure we were in different classrooms.

Initially, first grade wasn't much better. I had trouble reading. My dad told me that if I got an A in reading he would give me one hundred dollars. Wow! A hundred dollars. I got an A in reading and ever since I have been a very good reader. I had the same teacher in first and second grade, Mrs. Hume. In second grade she saw that I had real potential. I was tested for the GATE (gifted and talented) program and was enrolled in special advanced classes. I was feeling pretty good about myself.

In the summer before third grade, the Army relocated my family to Hawaii. My dad did some special training to become a child psychiatrist. I had my own shrink for a dad. Sometimes that was great, because he could hypnotize me to go to sleep; sometimes it was annoying because he would ask too many questions.

Although I did well in school, I didn't like it very much. Homework took me a long time; handwriting was hard for me; and I had a lot of trouble keeping organized. My book bag was always a mess, papers always seemed to fall out of my desk whenever I opened it and my room was a disaster area. My dad would get frustrated with me a lot. Everyday after school he'd ask me what I learned that day. I always said NOTHING, because I couldn't remember paying attention long enough to what was being taught. That made him mad, because he was paying for me to go to private school. He instituted the rule of having to report on at least one new thing I learned a day. It helped me pay attention for at least a little bit.

At school in Hawaii I had trouble with other kids. I was called a "haole" (a white person and foreigner in the land of the Asians and Hawaiians). It was the first time I experienced discrimination. There was a fat child named Taylor who used to harass me. He would get the other kids to try to beat me up. I was scared nearly everyday for the first half the year. My parents then enrolled me in Japanese Karate. In two years I worked hard and received a black belt. The kids stopped bothering me when I could defend myself. But even at karate there were times when it was hard to stay focused.

Overall, I loved living in Hawaii. During my free time I loved catching lizards. If you have ever been to Hawaii you know why. The lizards in Hawaii are very exotic and very fast.

After two years in Hawaii, we were transferred for his last time in the military. We moved to Barstow, California. Barstow is extremely hot and dry. It is right next to the Mojave Desert (the hottest place on Earth). While in Barstow, I did well in school. In fact, I got straight As (except for 1 B+) in the sixth grade. It was still hard for me, but I really liked my teacher and I wanted to do well. In Barstow, my youngest sister Katie was born. She was a real handful. She was lively, active, and strong willed.

Also, while I was in Barstow, my biological father Jim died. I went back to Michigan for the funeral. I didn't know Jim very well. With all of the moving I only saw him a couple of times. He was always very nice to me. The funeral was really hard for my grandparents. Even today, I have trouble putting my feelings about Jim's death into words.

After two years in Barstow, my dad got out of the Army so that we wouldn't have to move all of the time. We moved to northern California where my dad set up his medical practice. As I became a teenager things became much harder. Seventh and eighth grade were a struggle. A half an hour of homework would often take me two or three hours to do. I was distracted easily and had trouble staying on task. Writing was also very hard for me. Even though I could talk about what I thought, it was very hard for me to write it down. I really hated writing. During that time it seemed my parents were on my case a lot to get my school work done. They told me that I was very smart and that my grades didn't match my ability. That really frustrated me, because the harder I tried the worse it got. In the 8th grade my dad sent me to see a psychologist for some testing.

The doctor was pretty nice. He gave me a lot of tests; some of them were very easy and some were hard. The doctor told my parents that I probably had a learning disability (How could that be, I was tested as gifted in grammar school?). He also said that I should talk about my biological father's death. I wasn't sure what to talk about. This was all very confusing to me.

During this time things at home became even more tense. My little sister Katie was difficult to handle. She often seemed upset, she ran around the house, and my mom had to put a lock on her door so that she wouldn't tear her room up. My parents fought over me. My mom said I wasn't trying hard enough. My dad said that something must be wrong.

In 9th grade things really fell apart for me. I stopped doing home-work. I totally spaced out in class. I just stopped caring. My friends were much more important than school. Many of my friends did poorly in school and ended up in the continuation school for kids with problems. My parents were so upset with me for not trying harder that they threatened to send me away to boarding school. I told them I'd run away if they tried to do that. During that time, my dad was doing research with special brain studies in children and adults with something called Attention Deficit Disorder (ADD). Given the difficulties I had he decided to study my brain. He said the findings were very interesting. He said that when I tried to concentrate my brain turned off rather than turning on, which is what it is supposed to do. My feelings were right. The harder I tried the worse it got! My dad also said that I had trouble shifting my attention and that I would get locked into certain thoughts. Dad said it was the reason I was so stubborn. Given my problems and the results of the brain study my dad said that I had ADD.

I tried several medications before I found the right one. Some of the medications made me feel tired, some of them gave me headaches and one of them made my hands shake. When I found the right medication, which for me is Dexedrine, it helped me concentrate and made it easier for me to get my work done. My parents said it made a big difference, even though I couldn't always tell. Having ADD, I often forgot my medication. When I went for long spells without it, my grades really dropped. When I took the medication I did much better.

Tenth and eleventh grades were a little bit better than 9th, but I still hated school. I thought it was boring and largely irrelevant. I still fought with my parents over schoolwork. One day my dad came home and told me about the California High School Proficiency Exam (CHSPE). His niece had taken the exam and went to college two years early. This was a way for me to get to a higher level of education without having to suffer through another year of high school. I jumped on the opportunity and studied during the next few months for the test. The day of the test I was extremely nervous. After taking the test I felt good and thought that I had passed. After six weeks the results of the test finally came in. I had passed.

Finding out that I had passed made me feel great. I felt like I had a second chance and still could make something of myself. I then started to go to a Community College where I will continue to go until I get my associates degree. I will then transfer to a four year university. I'm still undecided on a major or a career, but I'm looking at many options. I know that I like working with people, rather than computers or other machinery.

Over the past few years I've grown up a lot and things look brighter for me. I really hope my story helps you to relate to me as you read this book.

Chapter 2:

What Is ADD?
Symptoms,
Subtypes,
Checklists,
How Do I Know If I have It?

Attention Deficit Disorder (ADD) is a physical disorder of the brain which affects many aspects of a person's life. Attention span difficulties, distractibility, impulsivity and restlessness are the cornerstone symptoms of this disorder. ADD used to be thought of as a disorder of hyperactive boys who outgrew it as they became teenagers. What we now know, is that **ADD affects millions of girls and women**, and that **most people do not outgrow it**. Most people diagnosed with ADD as children continue with symptoms into adulthood. It is estimated that ADD affects approximately 17 million people in the US.

There are two major types of ADD.

ADHD, or ADD with hyperactivity (classic ADD)
ADD, without hyperactivity (couch potatoes)

Through a great deal of research, however, some professionals feel that there are three additional types of this disorder. They can also occur in various combinations:

ADD, overfocused (tend to get stuck)
ADD, depressive (negative and irritable)
ADD, violent, explosive (dark thoughts)

Here are the major symptoms for the subtypes of ADD. Use the checklists to see which ones might apply to you. We have included the part of the brain suspected to be involved with each subtype in parentheses.

CRITERIA FOR
AD/HD
Attention-Deficit/Hyperactivity

(Prefrontal Cortex System)

Section 1 <u>or</u> 2 is needed for diagnosis

Section 1: six (or more) of the following symptoms of inattention have persisted for at least six months to a degree that is maladaptive and inconsistent with developmental level:

Inattention

_____ 1. often fails to give close attention to details or makes careless mistakes in schoolwork, work, or other activities

_____ 2. often has difficulty sustaining attention in tasks or play activities

_____ 3. often does not seem to listen when spoken to directly

_____ 4. often does not follow through on instructions and fails to finish schoolwork, chores, or duties in the workplace (not due to oppositional behavior or failure to understand instructions)

_____ 5. often has difficulty organizing tasks and activities

_____ 6. often avoids, dislikes, or is reluctant to engage in tasks that require sustained mental effort (such as schoolwork or homework)

_____ 7. often loses things necessary for tasks or activities (e.g., toys, school assignments, pencils, books, or tools)

_____ 8. is often easily distracted by extraneous stimuli

_____ 9. is often forgetful in daily activities

Section 2: **six (or more)** of the following symptoms of hyperactivity-impulsivity have persisted for at least six months to a degree that is maladaptive and inconsistent with developmental level:

Hyperactivity

____ 1. often fidgets with hands or feet or squirms in seat
____ 2. often leaves seat in classroom or in other situations in which remaining seated is expected
____ 3. often runs about or climbs excessively in situations in which it is inappropriate (in adolescents or adults, may be limited to subjective feelings of restlessness)
____ 4. often has difficulty playing or engaging in leisure activities quietly
____ 5. is often "on the go" or often acts as if "driven by a motor"
____ 6. often talks excessively

Impulsivity

____ 7. often blurts out answers before questions have been completed
____ 8. often has difficulty awaiting turn
____ 9. often interrupts or intrudes on others (e.g., butts into conversations or games)

The onset of at least some symptoms must have been before age seven and must have lasted for at least six months. In order to make the diagnosis, some impairment from the symptoms is required to be present in two or more settings (e.g., school [or work] and at home). There must also be clear evidence of clinically significant impairment in social, academic, or occupational functioning. The severity of the disorder is rated as mild, moderate or severe.

Based on DSM-IV criteria, there can be three subtypes:

AD/HD, combined type,
  if both criterion for 1 and 2 are met

AD/HD, predominantly inattentive type,
  if criterion 1 is met but criterion 2 is not

AD/HD, predominantly hyperactive-impulsive type,
  if criterion 2 is met but criterion 1 is not

The boys with AD/HD combined or predominantly hyperactive-impulsive type are often identified early in life. The level of hyperactivity, restlessness and impulsivity causes them to stand out from others. AD/HD predominantly inattentive type girls, on the other hand, may be ignored because they get labeled as "social butterflies." Even as we near the next century, societal expectations are different for girls than they are for boys.

Brain studies of patients with classic AD/HD reveal a decrease in brain activity in the frontal lobes of the brain in response to an intellectual challenge. The harder these people try to concentrate, the worse it gets.

Classic ADHD is usually very responsive to stimulant medications, such as Ritalin, Dexedrine, Cylert, Desoxyn, and Adderal. These medications "turn on" the frontal lobes and prevent the shutdown which often occurs with ADD.

HALLMARKS OF ADD without Hyperactivity
AD/HD, Predominantly Inattentive Type

(Prefrontal Cortex System)

Six or more of the following symptoms are indicative of ADD without hyperactivity.

_____ 1. Difficulty with sustained attention or erratic attention span
_____ 2. Easily distracted by extraneous stimuli
_____ 3. Excessive daydreaming
_____ 4. Disorganized
_____ 5. Responds impulsively or without thinking
_____ 6. Problems completing things
_____ 7. Doesn't seem to listen
_____ 8. Shifts from one uncompleted activity to another
_____ 9. Often complains of being bored
_____ 10. Often appears to be apathetic or unmotivated
_____ 11. Frequently sluggish or slow moving
_____ 12. Frequently spacy or internally preoccupied

The onset of these symptoms often becomes apparent later in childhood or even adolescence. The brighter the individual, the later symptoms seem to become a problem. The symptoms must be present for at least six months and not be related to a depressive episode. The severity of the disorder is rated as mild, moderate or severe.

Even though these children have many of the same symptoms of the people with AD/HD, they are not hyperactive and may, in fact, be hypoactive. Girls are frequently missed because they are more likely to have this type of ADD. In addition, they may: daydream excessively, complain of being bored, appear apathetic or unmotivated, appear frequently sluggish or slow moving or appear spacy or internally preoccupied -- the classic "couch potato." Most people with this form of ADD are never diagnosed. They do not exhibit enough symptoms that "grate" on the environment to cause people to seek help for them. Yet, they often experience severe disability from the disorder. Instead of help, they get labeled as willful, uninterested, or defiant.

As with the AD/HD subtype, brain studies in patients with ADD, inattentive subtype reveal a decrease in brain activity in the frontal lobes of the brain in response to an intellectual challenge. Again, it seems that the harder these people try to concentrate, the worse it gets. ADD, inattentive subtype is often very responsive to the stimulant medications previously listed, at a percentage somewhat less than the AD/HD patients.

HALLMARKS OF ADD
Overfocused Subtype

(Cingulate System)

Six or more of the following symptoms are indicative of ADD overfocused (1 and 2 are needed to make the diagnosis).

____ 1. Difficulty with sustained attention or erratic attention span
____ 2. Easily distracted by extraneous stimuli
____ 3. Excessive or senseless worrying
____ 4. Disorganized or super-organized
____ 5. Oppositional, argumentative
____ 6. Strong tendency to get locked into negative thoughts, having the same thought over and over
____ 7. Tendency toward compulsive behavior
____ 8. Intense dislike for change
____ 9. Tendency to hold grudges
____10. Trouble shifting attention from subject to subject
____11. Difficulties seeing options in situations
____12. Tendency to hold on to own opinion and not listen to others
____13. Tendency to get locked into a course of action, whether or not it is good for the person
____14. Needing to have things done a certain way or becomes very upset
____15. Others complain that you worry too much

People with ADD, overfocused subtype, tend to get locked into things and they have trouble shifting their attention from thought to thought. This subtype has a very specific brain pattern, showing increased blood flow in the top, middle portion of the frontal lobes.

This is the part of the brain that allows you to shift your attention from thing to thing. When this part of the brain is working too hard, people have trouble shifting their attention and end up "stuck" on thoughts or behaviors.

This brain pattern may present itself differently among family members. For example, a mother or father with ADD overfocused subtype may experience trouble focusing along with obsessive thoughts (repetitive negative thoughts) or have compulsive behaviors (hand washing, checking, counting, etc.). The son or daughter may be oppositional (get stuck on saying no, no way, never, you can't make me do it), and another family member may find change very hard for them.

This pattern is often very responsive to new "anti-obsessive antidepressants," which increase the neurotransmitter serotonin in the brain. I have nicknamed these medications as my "anti-stuck medications." These medications include Prozac, Paxil, Zoloft, Anafranil, Luvox and Effexor.

HALLMARKS OF ADD
Depressive Subtype

(Limbic System)

Six or more of the following symptoms are indicative of ADD depressive subtype (1 and 2 are needed to make the diagnosis).

____ 1. Difficulty with sustained attention or erratic attention span
____ 2. Easily distracted by extraneous stimuli
____ 3. Moodiness
____ 4. Negativity
____ 5. Low energy
____ 6. Irritability
____ 7. Social isolation
____ 8. Hopelessness, helplessness, excessive guilt
____ 9. Disorganization
____10. Lowered sexual interest
____11. Sleep changes (too much or too little)
____12. Forgetfulness
____13. Low self-esteem

It is very important to differentiate this subtype of ADD from clinical depression. This is best done by evaluating the symptoms over time. ADD, depressive subtype, is consistent over time and there must have been evidence from childhood and adolescence. It does not just show up at the age of 35 when someone is going through serious stress in their life. It must be a pattern of behavior over time. Major depressive disorders tend to cycle. There are periods of normalcy which alternate with periods of depression.

The medications used for ADD, depressive subtype include standard antidepressants, such as Tofranil (imipramine), Norpramin (desipramine), and Pamelor (nortryptiline), the newer antidepressants such as Prozac and Wellbutrin (buprion), and the stimulants. Clinically, I have been very impressed with the ability of stimulants to help this subtype of ADD. This is why it is very important to differentiate this subtype from primary depressive disorders.

HALLMARKS OF ADD
Explosive Subtype

(Temporal Lobe Subtype)

Six or more of the following symptoms are indicative of ADD violent, explosive subtype (1 and 2 are needed to make the diagnosis).

____ 1. Difficulty with sustained attention or erratic attention span

____ 2. Easily distracted by extraneous stimuli

____ 3. Impulse control problems

____ 4. Short fuse or periods of extreme irritability

____ 5. Periods of rages with little provocation

____ 6. Often misinterprets comments as negative when they are not

____ 7. Irritability builds, then explodes, then recedes; often tired after a rage

____ 8. Periods of spaciness or confusion

____ 9. Periods of panic or fear for no specific reason

____10. Visual changes, such as seeing shadows or objects changing shape

____11. Frequent periods of deja vu (feelings of being somewhere before even though you never have)

____12. Sensitivity or mild paranoia

____13. History of a head injury or family history of violence or explosiveness

____14. Dark thoughts; may involve suicidal or homicidal thoughts

____15. Periods of forgetfulness or memory problems

In my clinical experience, temporal lobe symptoms are found in approximately 10-15% of patients with ADD. Temporal lobe symptoms can be among the most painful. These include periods of panic or fear for no specific reason, periods of spaciness or confusion, dark thoughts (such as suicidal or homicidal thoughts), significant social withdrawal, frequent periods of deja vu, irritability, rages, and visual changes (such as things getting bigger or smaller than they really are). Temporal lobe dysfunction may be inherited or it may be caused by some sort of brain trauma.

Temporal lobe symptoms associated with ADD are often very responsive to antiseizure medications, such as Tegretol or Depakote.

Overview and Additional Symptoms Of ADHD:

1. Restless, fidgety
-- like a mosquito buzzing around the environment, or
-- a bullet ricocheting off the walls,
-- jitterbug, others note excessive movement
-- legs or fingers in constant motion
-- hyperactivity

2. Problems remaining seated
-- up, down, all around
-- swinging around in seat
-- constantly up

3. Easily distracted by extraneous stimuli
-- trouble remaining focused
-- hears whatever else is going on
-- if someone drops a pencil three rows over, their attention immediately goes to the pencil and distracts them from their task

4. Problems taking turns
-- need to have way immediately
-- often tries to cut to the front of the line
-- alienates themselves socially from others

5. Responds impulsively or without thinking
-- most people have a little brake in their brain that causes them to think before they act; people with ADD seem to be missing that brake and react often without forethought

6. Problems completing things
  -- homework, school work, chores
  -- start many things that they do not finish

7. Difficulty with sustained attention or erratic attention
  -- short attention span for most things
  -- people with ADD may be able to concentrate on things that are
      new (sitting in the pediatrician's office), novel, highly
      interesting (video games) or frightening (dad coming home
      from work after mom has called him out of a meeting)

8. Shifts from one uncompleted activity to another
  -- with a short attention span, the ADD person often will go from
      activity to activity, toy to toy or project to project

9. Difficulty playing quietly
  -- often described as noisy, loud or intrusive (this may be very
      difficult for a mother who is sensitive to noise)

10. Talks excessively
  -- phrases such as "motor mouth," or "who put a quarter in you" are
      often heard with these people

11. Interrupts frequently
  -- blurts out answers in class even after being warned not to time
      after time. Often this is upsetting and embarrassing for parents

12. Doesn't seem to listen
  -- this may seem somewhat selective, people with ADD often
      absorb less than 30% of what is said, causing misperception
      and misinterpretation

13. Disorganization

  -- problems with managing book bags, homework, bedrooms, desks, offices, and paperwork are very common with these children.

  -- an inability to manage time (often late or in a hurry) and an overall problem with organization is also common.

14. Takes high risks

  -- these children are at risk for accidents (running into the street without thinking, getting hold of medication that is left out, climbing up cupboards or on top of appliances, etc.)

Additional Symptoms

-- often poor handwriting; as adults, they may print
-- trouble writing, even though they may be able to say what they are thinking. They have trouble writing what they are thinking (this has been termed finger agnosia)
-- often have difficulty getting to sleep and have trouble getting up in the morning
-- cannot tune out the edges and concentrate on the middle
-- poor memory, scattered
-- poor follow through
-- homework takes forever
-- they tend to be very stimulation-seeking and are experts at getting others angry at them
-- easily frustrated
-- poor eye tracking
-- poor self-esteem, especially with late diagnosis
-- chronic failure to master social and academic situations
-- unpleasant reaction from others due to their behavior
-- suffer from an overdose of criticism

-- children are often demoralized and may look depressed
-- decreased coordination compared to peers
-- many have "soft neurological signs" such as fine motor problems

Chapter 3:

A.D.D. THROUGHOUT THE LIFECYCLE

Here's a look at ADD throughout the life cycle. It is important to note that ADD does not just show up in the teenage years or in adulthood. When you know what to look for, ADD symptoms have been present for most of the person's life.

-- many children are noted to be overly active in the womb (one mother told Dr. Amen that her unborn child broke her 9th rib from kicking her so hard)

-- many ADD children are difficult from birth, colicky, fussy eaters, have a difficult time being comforted, sensitive to noise and touch, eating and sleeping difficulties

-- as toddlers they're often excessively active, mischievous, demanding, difficult to toilet train and noncompliant with parental requests (it is like the terrible twos that are continued...)

-- most ADD children are first recognized in kindergarten, first or second grade; school teachers often notice the difference between these children and normal children

-- by the time an ADD child has entered school, problems with aggression, defiance and oppositional behavior have often emerged

-- the majority of ADD kids have varying degrees of poor school performance related to failure to finish assigned tasks, disruptive behavior during class and poor peer relations. The time that this happens often relates to intelligence and school setting. Often the brighter the child, the later he or she is diagnosed. Up until that time, the child is likely to be labeled as an underachiever, willful, defiant or oppositional.

-- many have significant learning disabilities in the area of reading, spelling, handwriting, math or language

-- as teenagers, approximately 25% outgrow symptoms

-- most do not outgrow their symptoms at puberty, as previously thought, and have difficulty with their family, school or the community!!

-- high incidence of family conflicts, these conflicts often center around failure to perform routine chores, difficulty being trusted to obey the rules, and high levels of conflicts with parents

-- up to 30% fail to finish high school, many bright people fail to pursue college

-- as adults, as many as 75% have interpersonal problems; depression and low self-esteem are commonplace

-- juvenile convictions and adult antisocial personality disorders may occur in 23-45%

-- 50% or more abuse alcohol and drugs, especially amphetamines and cocaine (possibly for self-medication)

Left untreated this disorder has serious consequences!!

WATCH FOR THE WALL

Many bright teens with ADD, especially the type without hyperactivity, are not diagnosed until later in their development. They do fine for a while and then slam into failure. The Wall! Depending on intelligence, class size and knowledge level of parents they may not have problems until third grade, sixth grade, ninth grade or even college. I've treated some college professors who received good grades in graduate school, but still had the majority of symptoms of the disorder. They describe, however, that it took them four or five times the amount of time and effort to do well as their peers.

AJA:

My greatest difficulties were in the ninth grade. I actually got straight As in the sixth grade. In sixth grade I knew everything that the teacher was talking about. It was easy. In ninth grade I did not know as much and I couldn't bring myself to focus on all the material I needed to learn. The WALL is different for each person with ADD.

Chapter 4:

WHAT CAUSES A.D.D.

There are many theories about what causes ADD. The following items seem to be the most well established causes at this time.

** high genetic transmission: (by far the most common, especially in families with a history of ADD, learning problems, depression, alcoholism or drug abuse)

** maternal alcohol or drug use (fetal alcohol/drug syndromes include short attention span, restlessness and impulsivity)

** birth problems (lack of oxygen at birth, jaundice, etc.)

** head trauma (sometimes even minor ones; head traumas affect learning and behavior)

** radiation exposure

** brain infections as a preschooler

** high fevers for more than 24 hours

WHY

** some researchers feel there are brain chemical problems with something called neurotransmitters which help your brain work efficiently. The neurotransmitters called "dopamine and norepinephrine" seem to be the most involved in classic ADD. The neurotransmitter called "serotonin" seems to be mostly involved in the overfocused ADD group.

** doctors have shown decreased blood flow in the frontal lobe of the brain (the area of the brain underneath your forehead, in the front)

** some researchers feel there is a weak arousal system in the brain and that hyperactivity is a way to turn the brain back on.

** for some with ADD, it seems that the brain fully matures later than for other people, which is why the symptoms for some people improve over time.

** Dr. Joel Lubar from the University of Tennessee has demonstrated that teenagers with ADD have different electrical or brainwave patterns than "normal" control teens. When the ADD teenagers try to concentrate, they get an increased amount of slow brain wave activity in their frontal lobes, instead of the usual increase in fast brain wave activity that is seen in the majority of the control group.

** In 1990, Dr. Alan Zametkin from the National Institutes of Mental Health published research on brain activity and ADD using very sophisticated brain imaging studies. He demonstrated that adults with ADD had decreased brain activity in their frontal lobes in response to an intellectual challenge, rather than the expected increase in activity that was seen in normal "control" adults. This finding was similar to Dr. Lubar's research.

The harder teens with ADD try to concentrate the worse it gets for them.

DIET AND A.D.D.

** some teens react negatively to certain foods such as,

  refined white sugar
  white wheat products
  milk
  certain fruits (grapes and grape products)
  caffeine
  chemical additives and dyes (mostly red and yellow)

Most studies report that less than 5% of ADD children, teens and adults are affected by food allergies. It is, however, often useful to pay attention to diet. If you notice a sensitivity reaction to any of the items listed above or any others, avoid them. It can make a difference.

How The Diagnosis Is Made

Assessment Tools

-- The history (interviews with children, parents, teachers and caregivers; for adults it may be important to talk with parents, spouses, lovers and business partners).

-- Behavior rating scales (such as the Conners Parent-Teacher Rating Scale for children and the Wender Scale for Adults) are often useful. The Conners is helpful in helping follow the response to treatment.

-- Psychological tests, such as the WISC-R, Matching Familiar Figures Test, Trails A&B Test, etc., can be helpful. There is, however, no one psychological test that is specific for ADD.

  Often, it is best for the psychologist to watch the patient's approach to the test, looking for clues such as impulsivity in responding, distractibility and a short attention span.

  Psychological and educational testing are often important, however, to help establish the presence or absence of concurrent learning disabilities.

-- Continuous performance tasks, such as the T.O.V.A developed by Lawrence Greenhill or the C.P.T. developed by Keith Conners, Ph.D., are another way to measure attention span and impulsivity. In these tests, you watch a computer screen and respond to appropriate signals. Prolonged response time, missed responses or incorrect responses often correlate with ADD.

-- Brain imaging studies have increased in use over the past several years, especially because the advancement in computer technology has allowed the price of the equipment to become much more affordable to local physicians and hospitals. Computerized EEG studies have been used by Joel Lubar, Ph.D. at the University of Tennessee and Dr. Amen has developed the use of brain SPECT imaging in ADD in Northern California.

Chapter 5:

Accepting A.D.D.

There is good news and bad news for those diagnosed with ADD. The bad news is that no one wants to have anything the matter with them. No one wants to be different or to have any kind of handicap. The good news is that ADD is a highly treatable disorder! Effective treatment often makes a major difference in the life of a teenager (and his or her family). We know teens who have gone from D's and F's in school to getting all A's and B's. We also know teens who have had horrible family problems that completely turned around when they (and their family) were treated for ADD.

One of the major problems for teens with ADD is to accept that they have a disorder. As we said above, no one wants to have anything the matter with him or her. Many ADD teenagers are very defensive. Often, they have been in trouble for so long that they deny that they have any problems.

Many ADD teens also have a strong tendency to BLAME their problems on other people. Their level of frustration causes them to blame their problems on others, such as:

"lousy teachers,"
"parents who expect too much from them,"
"inconsiderate friends," or
"brothers and sisters."

There are serious problems with blaming other people for the problems in your life. When you blame others you see yourself as a victim and you have no power to change anything in your life.

For example, if you say that you are doing poorly in Algebra because the teacher is lousy, then you feel that there is nothing you can do to change the situation and you are more likely to do poorly in the class. If you take personal responsibility for doing well in the class despite having a difficult teacher, then you will ask for help, making it more likely you'll do well in the class.

In properly treating ADD, it is critical to accept that you have it. When you accept that you have ADD, you are more likely to follow through with the treatment. Because of the problem with denial (no one wants to be different), many teenagers resist treatment. Unless you believe and understand the diagnosis, you may not take your medication as it is prescribed, or participate in the other forms of treatment. Getting well requires you to accept the problem.

Teens with ADD are not the only ones who have problems with denial. Many teenagers who have other medical problems also have trouble admitting the problem and following through with treatment. For example, many teenagers with diabetes (a serious blood sugar problem), do not follow their diets or take their medication as prescribed. Many diabetic kids end up in the hospital or in a coma because of their denial.

In accepting the diagnosis of ADD it is often helpful to look at the big picture. ADD runs in families. It is a genetic disorder. If you have ADD, it is likely that other people in your family have it as well. ADD exists over time. It is not something that just pops up at age 15. You can see evidence of it all the way along. ADD has a negative impact on a person's life. You can see problems associated with the symptoms of ADD.

In order to overcome ADD it is essential to see that there are problems, to want things to be better and to comply with treatment. Some teens who have ADD are afraid to get better. They are so used to having problems that they resist change.

Bill, age 16, had problems in school. He was impulsive, restless, distractible, and disorganized. He had problems in school for several years. When he went for an evaluation he was diagnosed with ADD. The doctor put him on medication and wanted to see him in psychotherapy. Bill tried the medication for several weeks. It was helpful for him. He could concentrate better, and his follow through on his assignments was better. However, he refused to see the doctor and he stopped his medication. He said, "There is nothing wrong with me. I just don't like school." Unfortunately, Bill had to fail several more semesters before he was able to admit he had a problem.

Admitting you have a problem and asking for help is the key to becoming mature and overcoming difficulties.

Chapter 6:

ADVANTAGES OF A.D.D.

Is there anything good about having ADD? Yes!! Many people with ADD have wonderful traits and abilities that often get overlooked.

Here's a list:

• Flexibility: many teens with ADD are flexible, and they may be able to adapt to different situations.

• Intelligence: even though they don't feel like it, many teens with ADD are very smart.

• Creativity: many teens with ADD are able to see traditional things in untraditional ways. They can often come up with new ideas or solutions for difficult situations.

•Intuition: many teens with ADD have good intuition and they are able to relate to people who struggle

• High energy and spontaneity: many teens with ADD have a lot of energy, they are able to "live in the moment," be spontaneous, and they are fun to be around.

• Lots of ideas: many teens with ADD have lots and lots of ideas. In business they are successful if they can surround themselves with people who help them organize their ideas.

"Things may come to those who wait, but only the things left from those who hustle.

Abraham Lincoln

PART II.

DEALING
WITH A.D.D.
DAY-TO-DAY

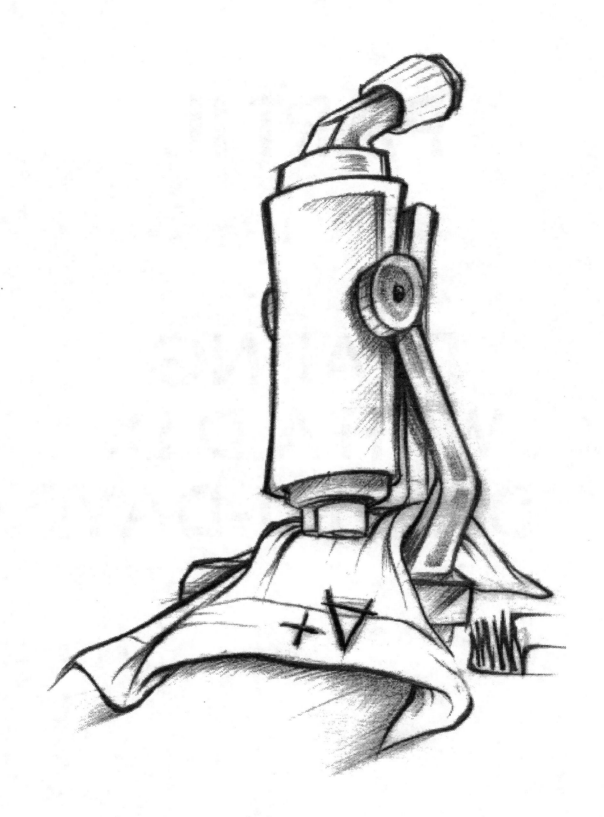

... AND THE YEAR GOES BY

"Hi little girl, you are defiant, strong willed, and an unruly scholar,"
I tiptoe into class without wanting to get noticed.
"OOPS," the teacher points. "Look who's late AGAIN."
I stumble into my chair, "Uh-oh. Where's my English book? Who
cares. It's just another referral in the trash can. Now I can go hide
and write on a more interesting topic than Emily Dickinson."

"Oh, sweetie, was that a joint in your mouth?"
"Nah, mom. I'm burning an exotic plant, that's all."

The teacher says, "Maybe you are stupid."
There goes my self confidence. I waved as it went "bye-bye".

Pointed out, I cried alone in my room. Am I hated? Am I wrong?
Maybe I was meant to be this way. God is cruel to me. Me. I'm sin-
gled out again as you point your finger to me.

Discriminations. Are my clothes too loud? Do you have a problem
with plaid and print together? Mismatched makes your tonsils curl.

I'm glad I don't have any tonsils.

I have no problem writing.
It's my business.
I'll do it right in front of your eyes.

The most angering words are, "Have you had your pills today?"
As I sheepishly say, "I forgot."

I'll admit I'm easily distracted. I always have a song in my head,
although I may not know the words.

I admit, I'm obsessed with talking.
What's quiet?
Quiet is something that involves listening to the Dead Kennedys
and typing my novel at 3 in the morning.
"Sorry, mom. I meant to wake up before your lunch break--
Oh yeah, we have dogs. They need to be put out."

Excuse me. I have a one track mind.
I'm going to skate, no write, no SKATE.

Vanessa

Chapter 7:

I'll Do It Later
How A.D.D. Affects School and Learning

"I hate school."
"School is boring."
"I can't get into it."
"It's too much work."
"I can't stay focused."
"Everything distracts me."
"It's the lousy teacher's fault."
"I left my homework in my locker."
"I'll do my homework later."
"I have two weeks to do it."
"I'm already failing. It's too late."

These are common phrases about school by teenagers with ADD. Procrastination, boredom, impulsiveness, restlessness, turmoil with teachers and forgetfulness are only a few of the problems that get in the way of a teenager's ability to succeed in school. Teenagers who may be very smart have trouble living up to their potential. This often causes frustration in the teenager, the parents, and the teachers.

Josh, 16, hated school. He was cutting classes, hanging out with kids who didn't care about school and constantly fighting with his parents. When he went to class he felt bored, tired and unmotivated. He didn't want to learn things that did not directly relate to his day-to-day life. There would be days when he really wanted to do well (mostly to get everyone off his back), but it seemed the harder he tried the worse it got. His mind wandered in class, he got distracted easily, and even when he did his homework he often forgot to turn it in.

One day, while his English teacher was lecturing, Josh turned around to talk with his friend who sat behind him. The teacher, who was irritated with Josh (because he only came to class sporadically and disrupted the class when he did) told Josh to either turn around and pay attention or leave and not come back. Josh told the teacher to go to hell and he left the class. The teacher called his parents that night. The parents, at the end of their rope with Josh, brought him to a psychiatrist for an evaluation.

Josh had been a very good student in the early grades. He was even tested for the GATE program in second grade. When he was pushed harder to concentrate in fourth and fifth grade things started to fall apart for him. Now in 10th grade, he was failing almost every subject in school. He hated school, hated his parents for hassling him about school, and he had little hope for his future. After he was evaluated, he was found to have ADD. Because he was placed on medication and seen in therapy for a few months, he was able to start to turn his life around. He even took English the next year from the same teacher who had kicked him out of class, and PASSED!
Like Josh, many people with ADD have significant problems with school.

Here is a list of common school problems:

Restlessness

The hyperactivity that often accompanies ADD may cause obvious problems: the teenager may be restless, out of his or her seat, irritating other people in class (not to mention the teacher) and causing turmoil and disruption. Others are often distracted by the constant movements (i.e., legs shaking, shifting body posture in seats, taping fingers, pencils, etc.).

SRJ:

When I was in fifth grade, I sat next to a boy named Chris. Chris and I sat together in the back of the room at a table. I'm still not sure why our teacher put two distractible kids next to each other. Chris was always moving during class. That year we were introduced to those wonderful and exciting things called lectures. Chris would get up at least five times during a lecture to sharpen his pencil. The teacher then restricted Chris from sharpening anything during class. Chris then took on a new habit of tapping his unsharpened pencils on the table. Then the teacher took away all of his pens, pencils, rulers, or anything else that was tappable. Chris then went on to tap his fingers on the chair or hit his knees under the table. Finally, Chris had to sit on the floor by the teacher in the front of the room. Still, he invented new ways to fidget.

Short Attention Span and Distractibility

Having a short attention span and being easily distracted are hallmarks of ADD. These 2 symptoms affect nearly every aspect of school. This may affect a teenager's ability to follow lectures, stay focused in small groups or perform consistently on tests. The short attention span often causes a teenager's mind to wander while reading or doing class assignments. This leads to assignments taking an excessive amount of time to finish. Distractibility also may get ADD students in trouble, as they tend to be in everyone else's business.

Distractibility can also lead to homework problems. Fourteen-year-old Jenny struggled with homework. Homework, which should have taken her an hour to complete, often took her three to four hours. Here's a typical scenario. She would sit down at her desk, spread out her papers, and then remember she needed to call a friend. When she got off the phone, she often would feel hungry and go downstairs to get something to eat. While she was downstairs, if her younger brother was watching cartoons she might sit down to watch a few minutes of it. When her mother yelled at her to get back to work, Jenny would feel picked on and started fighting with her mother. This went on year after year.

Sometimes the issue of attention span can fool professionals evaluating ADD. For things that are new, novel, interesting, highly stimulating or frightening, teenagers with ADD can concentrate just fine. Teenagers with ADD often do well at things like video games (which are new, novel, and highly interesting). It is the regular, routine, everyday, boring tasks (such as homework or chores) that give teenagers with ADD the most trouble.

Impulsiveness

Impulsiveness causes serious school problems. Blurting out answers in class, responding impulsively on quizzes or tests and saying things without thinking are typical of many teenagers with

ADD. Many teenagers with ADD are "tactless" in how they respond to their teachers or professors.

SRJ:

Courtney, who was in my sophomore history class, never hesitated to speak her mind. When our teacher, Mr. Golden, would say something, Courtney often had a thoughtless comeback. Things would really get bad when Mr. Golden would say something Courtney disagreed with. I remember one day during a class discussion when Mr. Golden was going on and on. He wasn't letting anyone else talk. He then asked the class, "Is anyone going to join in on this conversation?" Without a second to spare, Courtney yelled out, "Maybe if you'd shut up for one second, someone else could talk!" Mr. Golden replied, "Oh I'm sorry Courtney did you have something to add to our discussion?" "Ya, that you're a fat pig and it's your discussion, not our's!!" Courtney exclaimed. Even though many teenagers might think the same thing that Courtney said to the teacher, most teens would keep their mouths shut. They don't want to hurt the teacher's feelings and harm their relationship. But with ADD, sometimes you engage your mouth before you engage your brain.

Procrastination

Many people with ADD wait until the last minute to complete their tasks for school. Often, if it isn't the night before an assignment is due they cannot get their brain stimulated enough to get their work done. Many parents constantly fight with their children or teens about starting projects early and working on them over time, rather than the night before! Procrastination causes the work to be done poorly or for it to be left undone or incomplete.

AJA:

For years, I would wait until the last minute to get things done. I'd put assignments off and then forget about them. It caused a lot of stress. My parents would be angry with me for procrastinating once again. I'd have to stay up half the night to finish the assignment. Then the next day I'd feel terrible. I remember one time when I needed to give a speech in class. I put it off until 10:30 the night before it was due. I couldn't think about what to talk about. When I asked my parents for help they told me they were going to bed. They had told me about a thousand times to ask for help several days before an assignment was due. I stayed up nearly all night to finish the speech. The next morning I nearly overslept and missed the class.

SRJ:

Attending a school with twenty five ADD students was an experience. Before a test the classroom would be full of students cramming as much information in their short term memory as possible. Hardly ever were the tests studied for in advance, not even the night before.

Trouble Shifting Attention

Some teenagers with ADD have trouble shifting their attention from thing to thing. They have a tendency to get "stuck" or overfocused. This can cause problems in a lecture. Getting stuck on an idea early in a lecture may cause you to miss a lot of the information. Taking notes for these students is often a disaster. Note taking requires constant shifts in attention: from paying attention to the lecture, to the paper, from the lecture to the paper, from the lecture to the paper, etc.

Often, teenagers who have trouble shifting their attention have a need to have things "just so" or they get upset. One teenager said that she had to copy her papers over and over until she got them just right. Her homework took her hours longer than it should have.

Getting stuck on negative thoughts can really hurt a student's performance. Out of frustration and poor performance many ADD students start to dislike particular teachers. If they get stuck on these negative thoughts they may completely stop working in the class and end up with a terrible grade. Watch out when you get locked into certain thoughts or behaviors.

Forgetfulness

Unless something is very important to you, if you're ADD, you're likely to forget it. Even if it is important, you might still forget it. Forgetfulness causes big problems in school and often upsets parents and teachers. Forgetting to bring home books, leaving clothes at school, and not turning in homework assignments that were completed are common complaints.

SRJ:

I know about forgetfulness! During my sophomore year I went to the library and checked out four books on ancient Egypt. Those four books sat in my desk drawer for eight months. It wasn't until the library finally sent me a letter asking for the books back that I remembered I had them. I then put the books in my car. They sat there for two more weeks before I finally brought them back. I went to the library at midnight so that no one would be there when I dropped them in the night slot. Two weeks later the library sent me a thank you note for returning the book along with an overdue bill for $240.00. My mother was furious and all I could say was, "I forgot!" I had to work off the money by doing yard work (weeding, cleaning up after the dogs, etc.) for $4.50 hour. I haven't had any overdue books since, partially because Contra Costa County took away my library card.

Learning Disabilities

Specific learning difficulties are very common in people with ADD. It is essential to recognize and treat these problems if a student is going to perform at his or her potential.

Common disabilities include:

• writing disabilities (getting a thought from the brain to the pencil),

• visual processing problems (trouble seeing what is actually there), and

• auditory processing problems (trouble accurately hearing what was said).

When additional learning disabilities are present in teens with ADD it is essential to get the appropriate help for them.

Questions To Ask In Evaluating Learning Disorders

Reading
How well do you read?
Do you like to read?
When you read, do you make mistakes like skipping words or lines or reading the same line twice?
Do you find that you don't remember what you read, even though you've read all the words?

Writing
How's your handwriting?
Spelling, grammar, punctuation?
Do you have trouble copying off the board?
Do you usually write in cursive or print?
Do you have trouble getting thoughts from your brain to the paper?

Math
Do you know your multiplication tables?
Do you switch numbers around?
Do you sometimes forget what you're supposed to be doing in the middle of a problem?

Sequencing
When you speak do you have trouble getting everything in the right order (switch words or ideas around)?
Tell me the months of the year.
Do you have trouble using the alphabet in order?
Do you have to start from the beginning each time?

Abstraction
Do you understand jokes when your friends tell them?

Do you sometimes get confused when people seem to say something, yet they tell you they meant something else?

Organization
What does your notebook (room, desk, locker, book bag) look like?
Are your papers organized or a mess?
Do you have multiple piles everywhere?
Do you have trouble organizing your thoughts or the facts you're learning into a whole concept?
Do you have trouble planning your time?

Memory
Do you find that you can learn something at night and then go to school the next day and forget what you have learned?
Do you sometimes forget what you're going to say right in the middle of saying it?

Language
When someone is speaking do you often have trouble keeping up or understanding what is being said?
Do you often misunderstand people and give the wrong answer?
Do you have problems finding the right words to use?

AJA:

I hate writing!! It is easy for me to talk about a certain subject, but when they ask me to write about it I'm sunk. Also, I used to feel very embarrassed about my handwriting. In 10th grade a teacher told me that my handwriting looked like that of a third grader.

Finger Agnosia

Do you struggle with the mechanics of writing or "when you try to write your brain becomes scrambled?" This is very common in people with ADD and occurs in part because the person has to concentrate so hard on the actual physical act of writing that they forget or are unable to formulate what they want to write. The term for this "writing disability" is finger agnosia.

Common symptoms of finger agnosia include:

-- messy handwriting,

-- trouble getting thoughts from the brain to the paper

-- staring at writing assignments for long periods of time

-- writing sentences that don't make sense

-- frequent spelling and grammatical errors

-- many erasures and corrections

-- timed writing assignments are particularly hard

-- printing rather than writing in cursive

Here are some helpful suggestions for dealing with finger agnosia:

-- print as often as possible (it's easier and uses less effort)

-- learn to type or use a computer word processor (Mavis' Teaches Typing is an excellent program for teens)

-- try out different types of pens and pencils to see which ones work best for you. Some are more help helpful than others.

-- break down assignments and long reports into parts, and work at them over time, rather than all at once (such as on the night before they are due)

-- before you do the actual writing project, write an outline of the assignment to help keep you on track

-- write down your ideas before worrying about spelling and grammar

-- whenever possible, dictate your answer or report first. This often helps you add ideas and substance to the article that would not have been present through writing alone

-- use a binder or organizer to keep your writing assignments together

-- writing work loads at work and school need to be appropriately modified

-- avoid timed situations; take tests orally if necessary

Unusual Study Habits

Many teens with ADD have unusual study habits. Most need a very quiet place to study. Some have trouble studying at home, because they hear all of the things that are going on. Other people with ADD need noise in order to study. Some teens need the TV or radio on, or they need some noise in order to keep themselves awake and focused.

One teen reported that he took 6 hours to get in one good hour of studying. At his desk he would organize his pencils, start dusting the area, and play with the paper clips, making them into different shapes. After an hour he would realize that he hadn't gotten anything done and he felt a lot of stress. The stress, however, didn't keep him on track. As a way to entertain himself, he would then interview imaginary people for their opinions on his study habits. Homework took forever!!

Disorganization

Disorganization often haunts teenagers with ADD. Their desks, book bags, lockers, binders are often a mess. The disorganization causes assignments to be missed or tests to not be studied for.

AJA:

When I was in the third grade my parents came to my classroom for back-to-school night. They didn't know where I sat. My dad saw this one desk that had all of the papers hanging over the sides. When he opened the desk he knew it was mine. My desks were always messy.

Also, my book bag used to be incredibly messy. I used the "stuff-it-in-and-forget-about-it" file system. Most of my papers were crinkled up. In order to find something I had to dump everything out.

71

You could find almost anything in my book bag, except my homework. Gum wrappers, old batteries, lunch from several weeks ago (yuk!). Whenever my mom would organize my book bag she'd get disgusted and yell at me for an hour.

Disorganization affects every aspect of school; from preparing for class and taking notes to getting assignments in on time and studying for tests. Teens with ADD need to constantly work to keep themselves and their work organized.

While studying, many ADD teens have their work spread all over their rooms. Because of the disorganization, they end up going from task to task and get little done.

Energy Cycle

Understanding your energy cycle is very important for teens with ADD. Many ADD teens feel groggy and spacy in the morning and pick up later in the day. Some do okay in the morning and their energy falls in the afternoon. Many teens have their peek of energy late in the evening. If you understand your best (and worst) times then you can arrange your schedule to fit your energy cycle.

SRJ:

I'm not a morning person! Whenever I had a difficult class early in the morning I did terrible in it. I learned to take the hardest subjects later in the day. It made a big difference.

Timed Situations

Timed testing situations are often a disaster for those teens with ADD. Whether it is short math "drill" exercises, classroom writing exercises, or testing situations the more time pressure there is the worse it tends to get. Many schools will allow a person with a learning disability to have extra time on tests, both at school and also at national tests like the SAT.

School Survival Skills

Finding the best study strategies is critical to success in school. Here's a review of some school "survival skills" that many teens have found helpful.

Finding The Best Teacher

-- the teacher is a major determining factor on how well the teen will do in school. Choose carefully!

-- look for teachers who understand ADD or are, at least, willing to learn about it.

-- look for teachers who will give regular feedback to the teen and his or her parents.

-- look for teachers who protect a teen's self-esteem and will not put him or her down in front of others. Singling out a teen who is different sets him or her up to be to be teased by their peers!

-- look for teachers who have clear and consistent rules, so that teens know what to expect.

-- look for teachers who cannot be manipulated easily and who are firm, yet kind.

-- look for teachers who will motivate and encourage the ADD teen.

-- look for teachers who have an exciting and stimulating presentation style, using multi-sensory teaching methods (sight, hearing and touch).

-- look for teachers who give directions slowly and clearly and are willing to repeat them if necessary and who will check to see if the ADD teen is following them correctly.

-- look for teachers who will make adaptations as necessary, such as decrease the amount of an assignment, allow more time for tasks, allow for the use of calculators, etc.

-- look for teachers who will not undermine the treatment you have with your doctor. Some uninformed teachers we know have had the nerve to tell teens or parents, "I'm really opposed to medication."

Classroom Environment

-- at times the teen may need to leave the class for mastering concepts or resource assistance.

-- usually it is best to sit up front near the teacher with your back to the rest of the students to decrease distractions.

-- reduce or minimize distractions (both audio and visual); do not sit near the air conditioner, heater, high traffic areas, doors or windows.

-- take cooling off periods if you get upset.

-- surround yourself with "good role models."

-- work in groups with other students who care about their work.

-- learn to ask for help. Many ADD teens feel stupid asking for help, because of how much they have messed up. Remember, teachers are there to help you.

-- allow for periods of time when you can walk around. The helps to get out the restlessness.

Pacing

-- adjust time for completion of projects.

-- allow frequent breaks, vary activities often.

-- *do only one assignment at a time.*

Increasing Attentiveness

-- make sure you take your medication so that it is maximally effective during your toughest classes.

-- keep your eyes focused on the person who is talking in class.

--when you find your mind wandering get up and walk around class if possible.

-- actively keep notes to help keep your mind focused on the lecture.

-- ask the teacher to gently reorient you if he or she notices your mind wandering.

-- increase your participation in lectures.

-- take classes that are highly interactive, interesting, novel and stimulating.

Materials Needed For School Survival

-- day planner to know when tests will be and when assignments are due.

-- tape recorder to tape classes where it is hard to keep up.

-- highlighted texts/study guides.

-- use supplementary materials as needed.

-- note taking assistance; obtain carbon copies of notes from other students.

-- typed notes from the teachers (if they will allow you to have a copy of their notes it may be very helpful).

-- calculators or computer word processors.

-- use adapted or simplified texts.

-- use graph paper for math problems, handwriting, etc.

Assignments

-- break large assignments into small pieces.

-- use computer word processors to avoid losing assignments, also use grammar and spell checkers.

-- read directions for assignments before beginning work.

Reinforcement and Follow Through

-- set up a reward system for yourself, when you finish an assignment allow yourself to play a game, get a snack or call a friend (but not until the task is completed).

-- use peer tutoring.

-- have the teacher repeat the instructions when you're not sure.

-- use before and after school tutoring when necessary.

-- have regular conferences with your teachers and parents to help keep you on track (these people want you to do well unless you've done something to alienate them).

Testing Adaptations

For some teens with ADD the following adaptations are often help-ful:

-- take the test orally (the teacher or aid reads the test to the student and the student replies verbally).

-- tape instructions for the test so that the teen can listen to the instructions over and over if needed.

-- have the test read to the teen when reading is a problem.

-- see if it is appropriate that your doctor write a recommendation for you to get more time on exams.

Grading

-- get extra credit when possible from projects that motivate you.

-- if you disagree with the answer to a question that was marked wrong on a test politely talk with the teacher. Teachers make mistakes and they are often willing to change answers if you can make a good case for your answer.

-- have a good attitude in class. If you are on the border between grades (such as a B or a C) a good attitude may swing your grade to the higher one, a bad attitude may do the opposite.

Taking the Nightmare out of Homework

-- have a "special" quiet spot without distractions in which to do homework.

-- break into short segments of about 15 to 20 minutes, interspersed with physical activity, set a timer to structure work periods.

-- daily check assignment sheets and notebooks from the teacher to stay on track.

-- continually work on good communication between home and school.

-- reward positive homework behavior in yourself.

-- if problems continue ask your parents or teacher to supervise your work and help you with organizational skills.

Useless and/or Harmful Strategies

-- tell yourself to try harder
   (remember, the harder you try the worse it gets)

-- try to be motivated with guilt (I should do this). Should statements often cause you to do the opposite.

-- only notice your negative characteristics or behaviors.

-- compare yourself to other students.

Dr. Amen's Story and 20 more tips

In high school, Dr. Amen felt inferior to many other students. He was mediocre at best getting mostly C's with some B's. In college and medical school he was nearly a straight A student and felt inferior to no one. What was the difference? Was it intelligence, motivation, better schools, better teachers? None of these. The difference was that he learned how to do school. In his experience, schools spent a lot of time teaching him material and little time teaching him how to learn. He had to learn those skills on his own. Yet, in medical school he was told that 90% of what he learned would be obsolete in 10 years. Teens need to learn "how to learn" rather than just memorizing facts. Here is a list of the 20 most important tips Dr. Amen learned about excelling in school.

1. The student must be personally responsible for his or her own education. It is too easy to blame a difficult school environment, a poor teacher, or rowdy kids for your problems. When you blame sources outside of yourself for your school problems you become a victim and have no power to make a change. Say to yourself, "This is my education and I'm going to make it the best ever."

2. Be focused on what you are doing in school. Make sure that you have clearly focused goals for your education. Don't do it for your parents. Do it for yourself. When students do not have clearly defined goals, they tend to drift into mediocrity. See where you want to be in 1 year, 5 years, 10 years down the line. If you do not know what you want to study, a good goal is to search for the areas that interest you most.

3. Consider the teacher your best ally. Too often students are afraid of teachers or develop an attitude against them. Teachers are your most important resource. Get to know them. Get on their good side. Learn as much as you can from them. In my experience 95% of teachers want to do an excellent job and they are willing to help you be your best. After all, if you learn the material they will have done a good job.

4. Read the class outline or syllabus as soon as you get them, then develop a master calendar of the major assignments and tests in the class. Organization will keep you on track.

5. Read the introductions and prefaces of your textbooks. These sections often tell you how to get the most from your books.

6. Go to class!! In Dr. Amen's experience more than 70% of the questions asked on tests come from material covered in class. Going to class allows you the opportunity to discuss the material and clarify things you don't readily understand. In addition, you have to go to class to have a relationship with the teacher.

7. Read the material that will be discussed in class before you go. This dramatically enhances learning in lectures.

8. Sit near the front. This helps you pay attention and lessens the chances you'll fall asleep.

9. When you get lost or become confused ask questions! Many, many students never ask their questions. They are afraid that the teacher or other students will think they are stupid. In fact, the opposite is usually true. If you're lost in a lecture the odds are that others are as well. You might actually be helping others by asking your question. The 18-40-60 Rule will help you overcome your fear of

asking questions. The rule says that when you're 18 you worry about what everyone is thinking about you; when you're 40 you don't give a damn about what anyone else is thinking about you; and when you're 60 you realize that no one has been thinking about you at all. People spend their days worrying and thinking about themselves, not you. Ask your questions. You need the answers.

10. Organize your time so that you can be ready for tests two or three days ahead of time. This prevents you having to cram for tests. Cramming is a very poor study technique because you forget most of what you learn when you cram a lot of knowledge into a short period of time.

11. Take good notes or copy the notes of someone who does. Review your notes within 24 hours of the class. This will dramatically increase your retention.

12. Make summary sheets for each class as you go along. On one or two pieces of paper put down the major ideas for each chapter or section you are studying. These summary sheets make studying for tests much easier.

13. Spend time with good students. Other people are contagious. If you spend time with students who don't much care about school, you're likely to lose motivation. When you spend time with good students who want to do well their enthusiasm is likely to rub off on you.

14. Spend some time studying with a partner (a good student partner). This will help you see the material from another person's point of view. It will also give you the opportunity to teach the other person what you know. If you can teach something well then you know it.

15. Never try to impress others by being the first one done on a test. It is much more impressive if you get the best grade. Take as long as you need on a test. Be careful. Check your work.

16. When taking essay tests, answer questions concisely. Unless, of course, you don't have any idea of the answer; at which point rambling on and on is much more helpful (somewhat like politicians do when they don't want to answer a question).

17. After a test check your answers. Learn from your mistakes. If you disagree with some of the answers marked wrong talk to the teacher. Most teachers will give you points for a question if you can make a decent argument on why you answered in the manner you did.

18. Use tutors whenever needed. Asking for extra help is a sign of intelligence not weakness! Many people shy away from help, somehow feeling stupid for asking. In fact, the opposite is true. The most successful students and business people ask for help when they don't know the answer.

19. Use outside summary books, journal articles and encyclopedias to further understand your subject. This is the information age. Use whatever helps you learn.

20. Don't allow failure to stop you. Many successful people have failed over and over in their lives. What sets them apart from the rest is that they learn from their failures to move their lives forward.

Chapter 8:

A.D.D. and
Drugs and Alcohol

Drug and alcohol abuse is much more common in teenagers and adults with ADD than in those people without ADD. It has been estimated that when people with ADD ARE NOT TREATED up to 40% of them will have problems with alcohol or drugs. The drugs people with ADD tend to abuse are:

• alcohol or marijuana, because they tend to settle the restlessness they feel inside, or

• cocaine or amphetamines, because they stimulate the brain and initially make a person feel more tuned in. In a recent study from Johns Hopkins it was shown that 38% of cocaine abusers had a clear history of ADD that was never treated.

Potentially, there are many serious problems with using drugs or alcohol for any person. When you have ADD, drug problems can be magnified.

SRJ:

When my life got to the point of complete frustration, I turned to drugs. I was thirteen and in seventh grade. Before then I was very much against drugs, and had never had the urge to try them. At the time, however, I was failing in my life and I needed an escape from reality. Marijuana was in my face. What I didn't realize at the time was that it was going to be a long escape. After just a few times smoking pot, I needed to be "HIGH" in order to be happy.

I started not to have much control over my life. I started not to care about the people who really mattered to me. I mostly cared about getting high.

When I was in eighth grade my parents found out that I had been smoking pot. They were hurt and disappointed. When I saw that my parents were upset I felt bad for a while and every time I got stoned I felt guilty. The guilt feelings soon wore off and I was getting high before, after, and during school, and even before I'd play sports.

In ninth grade I needed to smoke more pot in order to get the same high. With the increased amount of pot I felt paranoid. Halfway through the year, I went on a weekend camping trip and tried mushrooms. The whole time I was "FRYING" (the term used for people high on mushrooms) I only wanted to come down and be sober again. I had no control over my body and I hated it. I promised myself that I would never "SHROOM" again. I also decided to really cut back on smoking pot, and did.

The following year, I was a sophomore in a new school. I no longer woke up in the morning with my first thought being about getting high. The first couple of weeks that I was there I smoked pot a few times, but more to fit in than to get stoned. After the first month I was at my new school I was diagnosed with having ADD. My doctor put me on medication, and explained how dangerous drugs are especially when they are taken together with the medicine. After starting the medication and seeing my doctor a couple of times I no longer cared about using drugs. I actually started to care about myself! I only smoked pot twice after being put on medication and that was in the first month.

Throughout my life and with all the mistakes that I have made, doing drugs is by far my biggest fumble. It's one of the hardest things for me to talk about and I don't think that I'll ever outgrow the pain. If I had just hurt myself by doing drugs it wouldn't be so bad, but I hurt my parents who are very important to me (sorry mom and dad.) Finally, after all the years of using drugs I have control over my life and I'm not willing to give it up for anything, especially not to my worst enemy; DRUGS!

Marijuana can be a major problem for people with ADD

• Marijuana also suppresses brain activity, making it harder for people to think.

• Marijuana decreases short term memory. In fact, when Dr. Amen was in the military he lived in a room with 6 other guys. Five of them smoked pot regularly. He said that when he tried to talk to the guys who were loaded they would forget what they were saying half way through a sentence.

• Marijuana decreases motivation. Many people with ADD already have motivational problems, when you mix ADD and marijuana it becomes very hard to stay enthusiastic about school or work.

• Marijuana worsens learning problems. When people who have learning disabilities, such as reading or math problems, smoking marijuana makes things worse by causing brain processing problems.

• Marijuana also makes some people feel paranoid and decreases a person's desire for social interactions. Many people with ADD already have social problems. Pot only makes them worse.

• Marijuana may distort a person's sense of time or motion. For example, 2 hours may seem like a half an hour, causing teens to be late coming home or late to class; or driving 90 miles per hour may seem like you're going only 20 miles per hour.

• Marijuana often increases hunger, causing significant weight gain. Many people with ADD have problems with compulsive behavior. Marijuana often causes eating behavior to get out of control.

SRJ:

A friend of mine named Sue called me about two years ago for a ride to an Alateen meeting. When I agreed to give her a ride she asked me to stay for the meeting. I asked her why she went. She said, "After the meeting you'll understand everything."

When I went to the door of Sue's house her mother answered it, and yelled, "Sue your friend is here!" Sue came running down the stairs and said, "Bye mom I'll be home no later than 10:00" Her mom then said, "All right honey now you go have fun at the mall." When Sue and I got in the car I said, "Mall?" She replied, "My mom wouldn't understand." So I left that conversation alone.

At the meeting we all sat in a circle. Sue was the first one to talk. As soon as she started I knew it was her mother who was the alcoholic, and that talking about her mother was very hard for her. Her mother's drinking was not something that she was used to talking about. Sue said, "My mom isn't the only one with a problem. It's a bigger problem for me to sit there and watch her drink, than for her to drink and not even realize it."

Sue was diagnosed with ADD three years before the meeting. Before she was diagnosed she was in all kinds of trouble with school, drugs, and her parents. She looked back and realized that she started getting in trouble when her mom started drinking heavily. She said that she and her mom had always been very close. They could talk about anything, except alcohol. For the first few years Sue ignored her mom's drinking habit and really wasn't bothered by it. When she was diagnosed with ADD and got her own life together, her mom's drinking became much more of a problem for her. It became hard for Sue to talk to her mom anymore, because sometimes her mom didn't make sense or she fell asleep when Sue was talking to her.

Sue said that she's lived with the guilt of turning her mom into an alcoholic. "With my ADD I was such a hard child to raise. My mom had to go to school conferences because I had misbehaved in class. She fought with me for hours every night to get me to do my homework. She and my dad often got into fights over me. I felt like a bad child and that it was my fault that my mom was drinking." Sue said she was afraid that her mom would die from drinking too much and that she would have to live with the guilt of killing her mom for the rest of her life.

"I know I should be able to tell my mom how I feel about her drinking," she said, "but the one time I did confront her she said that it was none of my business. She didn't have a problem anyway, but that I did." Sue never again confronted her mom about drinking. She was scared her mom would say, "You're the one who turned me into this alcoholic, so deal with it like I dealt with all the crap you put me through." Sue said her father totally denied there was any problem, and her only two siblings moved out of the house as soon as they turned 18.

Sue finished what she said at the meeting by saying, "Every time I see my mom drink I get a lump in my throat, a pain in my chest, a feeling of guilt throughout my body, and I get really upset and mad. I am always thinking about my mom's problem. Whether I'm at school, or with my friends. I feel like it's affected my ability to do my best at a lot of things."

To end on a good note, I talked to Sue while we were writing this book. "My mom decided a year ago to stop drinking," she said. "Don't ask me why she stopped. I have no idea what got into her and I really don't care. As long as she's not drinking anymore I'm happy. I feel like a huge burden of guilt has been lifted off my back. Now I can talk to my mom about ANYTHING, even alcohol." If only all of life's tragic stories could turn out like this one!!

There are many problems with
using alcohol when you have ADD

• Alcohol is a brain suppressant. It decreases brain activity. Initially it makes you feel more relaxed. Using alcohol over time, however, decreases your ability to think, causes memory problems and it increases impulsivity. As we have said, one of the major problems with ADD is that when you try to concentrate your frontal lobes tend to shut down; shutting down your frontal lobes further with alcohol use will make it nearly impossible for you to sustain work over time.

• Alcohol use increases impulsivity. Ever see people when they're drunk?

• Alcohol is addictive. You begin to need it even when you don't want it. It begins to control your life.

• Alcohol causes major family, legal, social, school, work and health problems.

• Alcohol harms children when the mother uses it during pregnancy.

• Alcohol related accidents are the leading cause of death in teenagers.

• There are better ways to deal with ADD than with alcohol.

SRJ:

Lisa, Mike, and Troy, were all very good friends. Lisa was in my English class. She wasn't shy about telling the class she had ADD and that she used to be on Ritalin. She stopped her medication because she said that there was nothing the matter with her. Within six months of stopping her medication she was kicked out of her house for severely rebellious behavior. From other people I heard that Lisa, Mike and Troy started to do "hard" drugs, such as heroin, speed, and crank. One day in English Lisa started to vomit and her body began to twitch all over. She became white as a ghost. She slowly fell off her chair and by the time she hit the floor she was passed out. Within five minutes paramedics were surrounding her, giving her oxygen and putting her on a stretcher. She was taken to the hospital where she had to have her stomach pumped. She was in the hospital for five days. She never returned back to that school. I later found out that Lisa had taken an excessive amount of coke. Her two closest friends Mike and Troy were also expelled from the school and were put in juvenile hall for having mass amounts of cocaine in their lockers.

Two years ago I met Ryan and Alex. They were both good friends of mine. When they were young both of them had been diagnosed with ADD, but their parents did not want them to take medicine. They both smoked pot periodically, but never around me. They started to smoke pot more often and I began seeing less and less of them. They eventually got to the point they couldn't live without it. I only saw them around school. They hardly would ever show up to school and when they did they'd get in trouble for picking fights, urinating in the middle of the halls, and if they weren't disrupting the class they were bugging students.

Ryan was kicked out of his house and went to live with Alex and Alex's grandparents. Alex's parents moved to Oregon and Alex wanted to stay and finish school. Both Alex and Ryan started doing cocaine. They both were kicked out of school for dealing drugs. They were now in trouble with the police, their parents, and the school because when they were kicked out they came back and vandalized it. They were no longer my friends but Ryan would sometimes call me. I asked Ryan once when he called, "Is this ever going to end? Haven't you learned your lesson yet?" He said "We're just having fun!" So I replied, "Well when you done having fun call me, but not until then."

Ryan didn't call for a year and when he finally did he said, "I think I've had enough fun to last me a life time, and I'm all done doing those

"FUN" things!" He was back living with his parents, had a job, and was going back to high school. All Ryan knew about Alex was that he was living with his parents in Oregon. I asked him, "What made you decide to get your life back in order?" He said, "I was in jail for eight months for dealing coke and having it in my system. I felt lucky for only having to be in there for eight months. Honestly I deserved more."

The last time I talked to Ryan he was still sober, had finished high school, was taking a full load of classes at CAL State and was playing on their football team. He said that the last he heard from Alex he was in a junior college and had a job.

The thing I really don't understand is why it takes so much pain and punishment to realize that drugs aren't for you, and really they are not for anyone.

There are many problems with using amphetamines or cocaine when you have ADD

Amphetamines and cocaine are very strong stimulants. They stimulate the brain. Even though on the surface these drugs are similar to some of the stimulant medications used to treat ADD they are really very different.

• Street amphetamines and cocaine are abused in doses 10-100 times stronger than the stimulant doses used to treat ADD.

• Street amphetamines or cocaine are not pure drugs. They are often made with substances like strychnine (a poison) to increase the feeling of a rush that abusers crave.

• Street amphetamines or cocaine are not used under the supervision of a doctor to help them understand the risks associated with them.

• Street amphetamines or cocaine potentially have serious side effects, such as high blood pressure, strokes and heart attacks. Stimulants used to treat ADD, in proper dosages, have few side effects and they are overall very safe medications.

• Street amphetamines and cocaine in high doses often cause paranoia. They cause you to feel that other people are out to hurt you.

Dr. A:

When I was in the military I once treated an Army Captain who was about to be promoted to the rank of Major. He started to use cocaine as a way to give himself more energy so that he could stay up later to do his work. After several weeks of using cocaine, however, he became paranoid. He started to think that his wife was having an affair. He became angry, irritable and very moody. After he used cocaine for several days he would then sleep for days at a time to recover. One day, after a run of using cocaine for several days straight, he seriously hurt his wife. He continued to believe that she was having an affair with a younger soldier even though she wasn't. When she denied his accusations he took out a knife and stabbed her several times. She was in the hospital for 3 months. He went to jail for 20 years.

• Street amphetamines or cocaine often cause serious withdrawal problems, especially with depression and suicidal tendencies.

There are also many problems with using hallucinogens when you have ADD (mushrooms, acid, angel dust, etc.)

Hallucinogens, drugs which alter your sensations and cause you to hallucinate, are often very serious drugs.

• Hallucinogens often cause distorted perceptions in any of the senses (sight, hearing, taste, touch, smell).

AJA:

I once had a friend who used acid before we went to the mall. While we were in a store that specialized in Troll Dolls he thought that the Trolls came to life and started to chase him. He ran out of the store yelling and screaming. I was never so embarrassed in my life.

•Hallucinogens may cause self-mutilating behavior.

AJA:

I also knew a girl who cut her arms open with a knife after she ate mushrooms. She told me that she wanted to see inside her veins.

SRJ:

I knew a girl whose use of acid turned violent. One night she was at a party with some friends using acid. After her boyfriend got off work he came to the party to pick her up. His parents were out of town and he took her home. They had sex and he rolled over and fell asleep. Because of the acid she couldn't sleep. While cuddling his body she got the idea in her head that she wanted to see what was inside the sac of his testicles. She went to the kitchen and got a pair of scissors and cut the sac between his testicles. He woke up screaming in pain, and then he passed out. When she saw all the blood she came to her senses and called 911.

• Hallucinogens may cause unpredictable behavior, severe panic attacks or depression, and feelings of being invulnerable (having the feeling you can fly, when you can't).

• Hallucinogens also may cause flashbacks of frightening experiences many years later. It also causes some people to see visual trails up to 20 or 30 years later.

There are many problems with using inhalants when you have ADD

Inhalants, such as gasoline, white out, paint thinner, lighter fluid, glue are also serious drugs of abuse. They are commonly abused by people with ADD as a way to get high or to forget their problems.

• Inhalants are addictive.

Dr. A:

I once had a four-year-old patient who had ADD. He also became addicted to inhalants. His mother told me that he would go into the garage, take the gas cap off the lawn mower, put his mouth over the opening and take a deep breath, becoming intoxicated with the fumes. His mother reported he inhaled many different substances even though she tried to supervise him. I first evaluated this child in the playroom of my office. He was very hyperactive! In the playroom I had a white marker board. During the middle of our session he went over to the board and took the top off a marker. He then put the marker up to his nose and inhaled deeply. He then gave me a big smile like "Yeah, this feels good." The scene gave me the creeps.

• Inhalants are directly processed into the brain and can cause brain damage, lung damage and liver damaged. These are dangerous drugs!

Other drugs of abuse include steroids, downers or depressants and pain killers. Like the other drugs listed they cause problems with motivation and concentration. Drugs limit your chances for success. How many successful drug addicts do you know?

Alcohol, drugs and ADD do not mix!

DA:

Robert, age 39, came to see me because he thought he had attention deficit disorder. He was forgetful, disorganized, impulsive and had a very short attention span. However, he did not have these problems in school growing up. They came on gradually during his adult life. Most notably, he also had a 20 year history of heroin abuse and he had been in multiple treatment settings. It is hard to describe my own personal feelings when I initially saw his SPECT study (see next page). This man was about my age, yet through abusing drugs his brain took on the functional pattern of someone 50 years older who had a dementia-like process.

This Is Your Brain

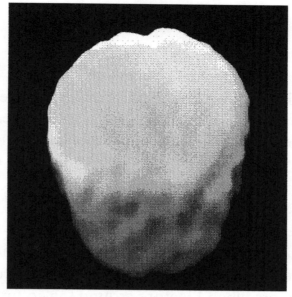

A healthy brain

This Is Your Brain
On Street Drugs

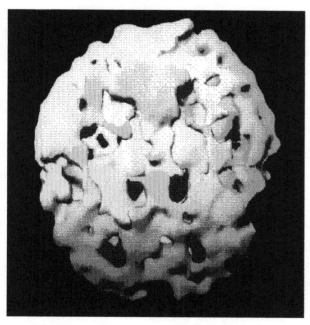

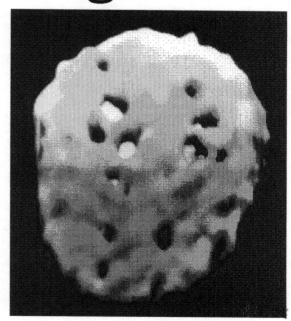

20 years of heroin

2 years of cocaine

Any Questions??

Images by Daniel G. Amen, M.D.

When I showed Robert his SPECT study he was horrified. Even though he tried to stop on multiple occasions to stop abusing heroin this time he went into treatment and was able to stop. Later he told me, "It was either the heroin or my brain. I wasn't giving any more of my brain to the drug."

Researchers are consistently finding that the effects of drug and alcohol abuse can cause serious damage to the brain. I often show Robert's pictures to the teenagers I see in my office, as well as to groups of teenagers when I lecture around the country. I find them more powerful than looking at fried eggs.

Alcohol, drugs and ADD do not mix! ADD, by itself, causes problems with short attention span, distractibility, restlessness, impulsivity and motivation. Mix that with any of these drugs and you are buying yourself real problems.

If you have a problem, stop using and get help. It may save your life.

Chapter 9:

The Impact of A.D.D. On Driving

An area that is often overlooked when discussing ADD is driving. Yet, this is a very important topic for ADD teenagers and their parents to consider. Think about it for a minute: if you take a teen who is restless, impulsive, distractible and somewhat stimulation seeking, and then put them behind the wheel of a vehicle which weighs several thousand pounds it could be a prescription for disaster.

AJA:

I know from personal experience the hazards of being ADD and driving. In the first three months I had my license I got into several problems, mostly when I forgot to take my medication. I had a couple of minor fender benders, but I didn't think much about it. Then one day my Bronco was in the shop. I had to borrow my dad's car, a little yellow 450SL Mercedes sports car which his father gave him as a present. I was with a friend and unfortunately had forgotten to take my medication (my first mistake). While I was driving I was drinking a 2-liter bottle of coke (my second mistake). With the radio going, I accidentally spilled the bottle of coke all over me which caused me to swerve into about 10 wooden poles and go off the road onto a golf course about 20 feet below (my third mistake). A crowd of golfers were around. I got panicked (this is more likely to happen off the medication) and drove the car up the side of the hill and down the street (my fourth mistake). I was scared to death. There was $6500 in damage to the car and at least that much damage to my emotional state worrying about what my dad was going to do to me. The incident taught me the power of cars, and the need to be more serious when I drive.

I have an ADD friend who often forgets to take his medication. He does stupid things with his car. One time he went to the top of a mud hill and slid his car down the hill. He acted like he had a four wheel drive vehicle, even though he only had a regular car. He broke off his exhaust pipe doing this stunt and his car sounded like a lawnmower for the next month until he paid to have a new exhaust pipe put on.

I have another ADD friend whose car caught on fire because he miswired his stereo. I told him I'd help him with it in a few days, but he decided he couldn't wait. He impulsively wired his stereo even though he didn't have any experience in it. He accidentally hooked up the car battery to an amplifier wrong which then caught on fire and caught the trunk, back seat and roof on fire. It cost him several thousand dollars to replace.

My dad told me about one of his ADD patients who got into an accident at 2AM. Even though he had car insurance, he fled the scene of the accident. He was arrested. Later he said that he just panicked. If he was thinking clearly he would have stayed at the scene. After all, he said, "I had car insurance. Nothing bad would have happened if I had just stayed there."

Drive safe. Live long.

Here are some helpful rules:

1. If you are going to drive take your medication, and make sure it is working whenever you're behind the wheel. This means if you are going to be out late then you may have to take a late dose. For example, if you take regular release Ritalin which only lasts 3-4 hours and you're going to be out until midnight, then you need to take a dose around 8 or 9PM. It may keep you up later, but your life is worth it.

2. Anticipate problems. Many teens are very defensive and they have a tendency to deny problems. Know that problems are possible and take extra precautions to be careful.

3. Don't be in a hurry. Too often teens (and adults) get tickets because they are racing to school or work. If you are a few minutes late, but get there alive and without a ticket, you'll feel better.

4. When you get experience driving you'll realize that there are a lot of bad drivers on the road. Drive defensively, be watchful, be careful.

5. Protect your driving record. Be more careful than daring. Insurance for most teens is expensive. When you get tickets or have accidents it becomes more expensive and can be prohibitive. Protecting your driving record will save you and your parents a lot of money.

6. Never drink or use drugs and drive!! If you are naturally restless, impulsive and distractible and then you add alcohol or drugs into your system it sets you up for major problems.

7. Always wear your seatbelt and make everyone else wears theirs as well. Many people with ADD just get in their car and go. Force yourself to develop the routine of putting on your seatbelt every time, no exceptions. Also, refuse to go unless your friends put on their seatbelts as well. Sometimes teens don't pressure their friends to do what is best for them, but if you are the driver you're in charge of the vehicle. Be responsible for yourself and the passengers.

Being able to drive is one of the most exciting privileges for teens. Protect the privilege, your friends, and yourself.

Chapter 10:

Getting Up/Going To Bed
How A.D.D. Affects Your Waking and Sleeping Cycle

Getting up in the morning and going to sleep at night can be real problems for people with ADD. We know this from personal experience!!

Getting Up

Mornings can be the worst. Here are some common statements teens say as they're trying to get out of bed:

"Later..."
"Just a few more minutes."
"I'll get up in a little bit."
"Leave me alone."
"My alarm is set." (even though it already went off)
"I'm too tired to get up."
"OK, I'm up." (only to lay back down for several hours)

Many people with ADD feel very groggy or fuzzy headed in the morning. The harder they try to get out of bed, the worse it gets. One teenager we know had such a hard time getting out of bed that she almost got fired from her summer job. Her boss told her if she was late one more time she was gone. She actually went to an alarm company and bought a siren to wake her up. She also had 3 alarm clocks and she had two of her friends call her in the morning. Many

Time to get up!

high school students have difficulty being late for school because of the trouble getting up. Adults with ADD also have this problem. Have you ever heard of adults who say that they have to have a couple cups of coffee in the morning to get going? Coffee contains the stimulant caffeine (stimulants are common treatment for ADD).

Parents complain that they have to wake up teenagers 3, 4, 5, 6, even 10 times before they get out of bed. This can cause a lot of family turmoil in the morning. When parents have to tell a teenager over and over to get out of bed, they can get pretty irritable. They may start yelling, threatening, or using force to get the teen moving. Some parents we know use water or ice to help the teenager get up. The marring grogginess causes many people with ADD to be frequently late, which stresses out everyone in the morning, especially if the parent has to get to work or has other children to get to school.

The teenager, who is woken up by the parent's hostility, starts the day off in a bad mood. It's hard to concentrate in class when you have just been yelled at, threatened or grounded because you couldn't get out of bed on time. This also leads to other problems for the teenager. For example, if you can't get up on time you may miss the bus, get a speeding ticket, end up in the tardy tank or just cut class so that you're not late again. Starting the day off on the wrong foot can affect your mood and attitude for the whole day.

Many teenagers say that when they get up on their own they tend to do better than if their parents are screaming at them. It often becomes a battle of wills, because the teen is angry that someone is nagging them. Both parent and teen end up feeling terrible.

Without parents hassling kids, some teenagers don't get out of bed until noon, 1, 2 or even 3 PM. This can cause serious problems.

When a teen gets up late, they will have trouble going to sleep at night. Getting up late causes a large part of the day to go by without participating in it. Many parents complain that their kids are wasting the day.

Helpful Hints For Getting Going In The AM

1. Go to bed at a reasonable time (see bedtime suggestions below).

2. Find an alarm clock that plays the kind of music that gets you going (some teens like fast rock music to wake them up, others like rap, some even like country music). Try different forms of music to see what works best for you. This beats having your parents stressed out. (You know stressed out parents often take it out on the teens.)

3. Keep the alarm clock (or clocks) across the room so that you have to get out of bed to turn them off. Don't have the kind of alarm that turns itself off after 30 seconds. Have one that keeps going, and going, and going.

4. Take your medicine a half an hour before you're supposed to get out of bed.

5. Have something that motivates you in the morning. Sometimes having your girlfriend or boyfriend call you can be great motivation. Some teens enjoy working out with weights in the morning as a way to get their bodies (and brains) feeling alive.

6. Stay away from early classes and early morning jobs if possible. In college, AA starts his classes at 10:00. He was often late when he took early morning classes which affected his performance (being

107

late also irritates teachers which is the last thing you want to do if you want to do well in school!)

7. Watch your own body's cycle. Some people are good in the morning and some later on. Fit your schedule to your body's rhythms.

Going To Bed

Many people with ADD have sleep problems. Some "go and go" all day until they drop from exhaustion. Others have difficulty getting asleep, they wake up frequently throughout the night, or they're hyper in their sleep and constantly on the move. The person who gets a restful night's sleep is more likely to be calmer in the morning. The ADD person, who is often very hard to wake up anyway, becomes even more difficult to wake up in the morning and is certainly more irritable with a poor night's sleep.

Here are some of the things teens have said about their sleep problems:

"I have to count sheep to get to sleep. The damn sheep are always talking to me."

"When I try to get to sleep all kinds of different thoughts come into my mind. It feels like my mind spins when I try to calm it down."

"I feel so restless at night. It's hard to settle down, even though I'm dead tired."

"The worries from the day go over and over in my head. I just can't shut my brain down."

"I have to sleep with a fan to drown out my thoughts. I need noise to calm down."

Sleep problems can cause many other problems. When you don't get enough sleep you're tired in the morning, making it even harder to get up (which is already a problem for teens with ADD). If it is hard to settle down at night it might make your parents mad (because they know too well about the morning problems) and cause fighting with them. Not getting enough sleep continues the cycle of feeling tired and wanting to sleep during the day.

One teenager had such trouble sleeping that he could never go to bed before three o'clock in the morning. This caused terrible problems because he couldn't get up in the morning and he had to drop out of school. This caused him to feel isolated from other people his age. He even went to the Stanford University Sleep Center for help with his problem. In the end, medication was needed to help his sleep cycle.

Doctors aren't sure why people with ADD have more sleep problems. Some doctors think it has to do with a brain chemical called serotonin. When there is not enough of this chemical sleep is more of a problem.

12 Ways To Get To Sleep

Here are ten ways to increase your serotonin and make it easier to go to sleep. No one suggestion will work for everyone, but keep trying new tactics until you find what works for your situation:

1. Eliminate television 1 - 2 hours before bedtime, especially any

program that may be overstimulating (the shows you most like). This includes news programs, as people with ADD tend to ruminate on the bad things that happened that day in their own world and the world at large.

2. Stimulating, active play should be eliminated for 1 - 2 hours before bedtime, such as wrestling, tickling, teasing, etc. Quiet activities are more helpful in the hours before bedtime, such as reading, drawing, or writing.

3. Some teens try to read themselves to sleep. This can be helpful. But read boring books. If you read action-packed thrillers or horror stories you're not likely to drift off into peaceful never-never land.

4. A warm, quiet bath is often helpful.

5. A bedtime back rub in bed may be soothing. Starting from the neck and working down in slow rhythmic strokes can be very relaxing. Some teenagers say that a foot massage is particularly helpful (although it may be hard to find someone to give you a foot massage if you haven't showered or taken a bath before bed).

6. Soft, slow music often helps people drift off to sleep. Instrumental music, as opposed to vocal, seems to be the most helpful. Some teens say that they need fast music in order to block out their thoughts. Use what works for you.

7. Nature sounds tapes (rain, thunder, ocean, rivers) can be very helpful. Others like the sound of fans.

8. Some teens say that restrictive bedding is helpful, such as a sleeping bag or being wrapped tightly in blankets.

9. A mixture of warm milk, a tablespoon of vanilla (not imitation vanilla, the real stuff), and a tablespoon of sugar can be very helpful. This increases serotonin to your brain and helps you sleep.

10. Dr. Amen makes a sleep tape which is made by a special sound machine that produces sound waves at the same frequency as a sleeping brain. The tape is played at bedtime and helps the brain "tune in" to a brain wave sleep state, which encourages a peaceful sleep (Call Dr. Amen's office).

11. Learn self-hypnosis. Self-hypnosis can be a powerful tool for many different reasons, including sleep. Here's a quick self-hypnosis course:

-- focus your eyes on a spot and count slowly to 20...let your eyes feel heavy as you count and close them as you get to 20.

-- take three or four very slow, deep breaths

-- tighten the muscles in your arms and legs and then let them relax.

-- imagine yourself walking down a staircase while you count backwards from 10 (this will give you the feeling of "going down" or becoming sleepy)

-- with all of your senses (sight, touch, hearing, taste, smelling) imagine a very sleepy scene, such as by a fire in a mountain cabin or in a sleeping bag at the beach.

12. Sometimes medications are needed if getting to sleep is a chronic problem. There are pros and cons to using medication sleep aides. On the positive side, medications tend to work quickly and

can help normalize a disturbed sleep pattern. On the negative side, medications can have side effects (such as grogginess in the morning) and you can become dependent on them if you take them for too long. It is best to think of medications for sleeping problems as a short term solution. *Use the other ideas first.*

The different medications doctors prescribe to help promote sleep include:

Over-the-counter medications (you can get these medications without a prescription): such as Benadryl, Unisom, Sominex, Execdrin PM, Nyquil, etc.

Some antidepressants, such as imipramine (Tofranil), amitrityline (Elavil), or trazodone (Desyrel) (trazodone is used only in females, in men it may cause painful erections that won't go away). Often these are used in very low doses to help promote sleep. They are helpful in people who have a tendency toward depression.

Certain blood pressure medications such as clonidine (Catapres). Clonidine is often used to calm down the restlessness or hyperactivity that often goes along with ADD.

Sleeping medications, such as temazepam (Restoril), triazolam (Halcion), zolpidem (Ambien), flurazepam (Dalman), estazolam (ProSom). These medications tend to lose their effectiveness after a few weeks. They should be used on a short term basis only.

Getting up and going to sleep can hinder the success of teenagers with ADD. Use the techniques in this chapter to help. Be persistent. If one technique doesn't work for you, don't give up...try others.

Chapter 11:

How To Be Organized

Many teens with ADD sabotage their chances for success by having a disorganized approach to their life. They approach situations and goals haphazardly, and then they wonder why things don't work out for them. Successful people are organized. Certainly, successful people are not all organized in the same way, but they know their own method of organization or, at least, they are in contact with someone who helps them organize the material important to them. Successful people have an organizational structure for themselves, their time and their tasks.

Unfortunately, organization is a bad word for many ADD teens. However, learning to organize yourself, your time and your tasks can make your life more profitable and much easier. Organizing yourself, at first, will take some time. If you're like most people with ADD, you just go from day to day accomplishing what you need to for that day and moving on to the next day.

Here are 22 prescriptions to organize your life.

1. Daily, weekly, monthly, yearly and even longer-range planning is essential to planning and organizing your life. Once you have a clear set of goals and plans in place, the organization will follow, if you attend to it. Develop clear goals, both short term and long term.

2. Take an inventory on how you spend your time. Success takes significant time and energy. Do you spend time doing repetitive things that have little meaning, like watching TV or playing video games? We know many teens who watch over twenty hours a week of TV or waste time on video games. Unless your big ambition in life is to be a TV writer or video game critic, we can't imagine any great return on that time investment. In fact, these activities turn off your mind and make it harder to think.

3. When you have free time, use it to your benefit. Waiting is a part of life, and you can regard it as wasted time, or as a gift of extra time. Whenever you go somewhere carry some work to get done in case the appointment is delayed. However you decide to spend your time, make it productive for you. Look at what you do now and ask yourself, "What benefit am I getting, or what benefit are others getting, from me spending my time in this manner?" If the answer is no benefit, find something more productive to do with that time.

A word of caution: don't assume we're anti-relaxation. Exercise, recreation and relaxation are essential to a balanced life. We all need our batteries recharged in order to function at peak efficiency. Be against wasting time. The more efficient you are with your time, the more time you actually have for relaxation.

4. "Budget" is another bad word for many teens. We're not that fond of it ourselves, but we know when we're unorganized with time or finances, a budget can help give us the structure we need to become organized.

Dr. A:

While I was in medical school, I had a friend who counseled students who were in financial trouble. Repeatedly, he helped these students budget their money. Instead of being a restricting or choking experience, he said for most students it was a freeing experience. The worry over money was less of an issue for them because they knew what they had coming in and where it was going. Plus, they always budgeted some fun money that they didn't have to feel guilty about spending.

5. Some of you will balk at such a systematized approach to life, but we submit that the more organized you are, the more time you'll actually have to be spontaneous and creative. Creativity is not enhanced by disarray; rather, it is enhanced by order.

6. Carry a notebook and a couple of pens with you wherever you go. Write down things you need to do and ideas as they come to you. At night, keep this notebook near your bed to write things that come to you in the middle of the night.

7. Schedule similar tasks together, such as errands, appointments, maintenance or phone calls.

8. Write down a time limit for the different tasks to be performed.

9. Consider your personal effectiveness cycle. If possible, schedule your most important activities for the hours when you are at your peak.

10. Don't get bogged down in low-value activities.

11. Learn to say "no." Spend your time doing things that are consistent with your goals.

12. Reward yourself with unscheduled time. Deliberately schedule a block of fun time in which you are not obligated to the clock.

13. Watch out for the great time thieves--procrastination, indecisiveness, regrets, fear of failure, and worry. Research shows that more than ninety percent of things people worry about never materialize.

14. Take the extra time to organize your work area on a regularly scheduled basis. Devote some time each week to organization. Otherwise procrastination will take over.

15. Use the FRAT system in organizing paper flow:

   File it
   Route it
   Action
   Throw it away

16. Prioritize your projects.

17. Make deadlines for yourself.

18. Keep TO DO lists and revise them on a regular basis.

19. Keep an appointment and planning book with you.

20. Use a portable cassette recorder to remember ideas throughout the day.

21. Break down large tasks into a series of smaller ones. Do a little each day on a certain project.

22. Use file folders, desk organizers and labeled storage boxes to organize your paperwork.

Procrastination: Eight Ways To Beat It

1. Consciously fight procrastination. The sooner you do it, the sooner it will be done. If you can do it now, then do it now.

2. Break down overwhelming tasks into small tasks. This happens on assembly lines every day. Remember, "A journey of a thousand miles begins with one step."

3. Do a start-up task now! Go to the next step you need to do to accomplish that goal and do it. Just getting started will increase your momentum.

4. Make a wager with someone. Use your competitive nature to your advantage.

5. Give yourself a reward. Tell yourself that after you finish a difficult task, you'll reward yourself with something special you want.

6. Do unpleasant tasks first. That way, you'll have the more pleasurable ones to look forward to. If you save the unpleasant tasks for last, you'll have little incentive to get to them.

7. Tell someone else the date that you'll finish by. Putting your word or reputation on the line is often an incentive to get started.

8. Think about how you'd feel once the task is done. Anticipating the sense of accomplishment will help spur you on.

Take the time to organize yourself and your time. It will be a good investment in yourself.

Chapter 12:

The Impact of A.D.D. in Families

ADD affects everyone in a family, whether or not they have it. ADD affects the relationship between the teenager and his or her parents, how brothers and sisters get along with each other, and even how parents get along with each other. ADD is a family disorder!

Because ADD remains largely undiagnosed, most families with ADD experience tremendous turmoil. Over half of the families who have teenagers with ADD are described as tense and full of conflict.

Some common reasons for family conflict related to ADD include:

> failure to follow through on chores,
> poor organization and messiness,
> poor grades,
> short tempers,
> selfishness, failure to see the needs of others,
> arguing, fighting, name calling
>   (conflict seeking behaviors),
> not listening,
> miscommunication, misunderstandings
> chronic lateness,
> lying,
> borrowing things from others without asking,

forgetfulness,
stubbornness/inflexibility
  (needing to have things your way),
impulse control problem and,
interrupting in conversations.

We know many teenagers who have been sent to live away from the family as a way to eliminate some of the stress in the house.

Parents

How parents react to teenagers with ADD often depends on whether or not they have ADD themselves. Parents who have ADD themselves can be more understanding of the teens problems or shortcomings. They have similar experiences of frustration and failure which help them relate. Often the parents who do not have ADD have trouble understanding why their teenager has so much trouble following through on tasks.

On the other hand, parents who have ADD (and are not being treated) are often restless, irritable, conflict seeking, disorganized and may be explosive. They may say one thing one day and something else a few days later. Their unpredictability is often confusing to the child or teenager. Parents who don't have ADD are often better able to follow through on parenting issues, they tend to be more predictable and less emotional. When an ADD parent tries to help an ADD teen with their homework real problems can occur.

It is important for teens with ADD to understand that their parents have to deal with many of their own emotional frustrations. Parents see a child's performance as a reflection of their own parenting skills. When teens aren't working up to their potential parents feel they have done something wrong or that they are lousy parents. Because of this emotional tension, parents are often angry and, may take out their frustration on the people in their family. When the parent with ADD finds out that it runs in families they often feel guilty that they have given it to their children. This sense of guilt also may increase tension or negativity in the family.

Teens with ADD may cause parent-to-parent frustrations. For example, right before bedtime, the parents may be hoping for affection from each other. Then an ADD teen says something impulsive, doesn't do a chore, or in some way provokes turmoil, causing one of the parents to sexually turn off. This can cause serious resentment in the other parent, which can increase the amount of tension in the family.

Here are common feelings experienced by the parents of ADD teenagers.

Denial -- "There's nothing wrong with the teenager! He's only lazy, willful, oppositional, 'a bad apple.'" Or they may say, "He only needs more time, more attention, more discipline, more love, better teachers, a better school, or better friends." These are common excuses parents make to deny that any problem exists. Admitting that there is a problem is often so painful that many parents go years and years without seeking help. Denial can seriously harm a child's or teen's chance for success!

Grief -- There is often a grieving process that occurs in a family with an untreated ADD person. The parents or spouse often feel the loss of having a "normal" teen and end up feeling very sad that the situation is not as they expected it would be.

On Guard -- For many parents, living with an ADD teen is like being in a war zone. They have to be constantly on guard that the teen won't be in trouble at school, in trouble in the neighborhood or in trouble with the law. This chronic watchfulness causes much internal tension for parents.

Guilt -- Guilt is a significant issue for many parents of ADD teenagers. The turmoil that an ADD teen causes often brings on bad feelings. Parents are not "supposed" to have bad feelings toward people they love and so they end up burdened by feelings of guilt.

Anger -- Feelings of anger at the teachers, doctors, and the other parent are common in parents with an ADD teen. The levels of frustration are so high in these families that people look for someone to blow off steam.

Envy -- "Why can't we have normal kids? We didn't do anything to deserve the turmoil. It's not fair."

Blame -- "You spoil him. How's he ever going to learn if you do everything for him? You're too soft on her. You never say a kind word to him. If only you would be home more then we wouldn't have these problems with her." Blame is very destructive and rarely if ever helpful. Yet, it is all too common in ADD families.

Isolation -- "Everyone thinks I'm a bad parent. No one else has these problems. I can't go anywhere with him, I'm stuck at home." Feelings of isolation are very common. Many parents of ADD teens feel that they are the only ones in the world who have these problems. Joining a support group can be very helpful for these people.

Bargaining -- "Maybe she'll be ok if we put her in a new school. Maybe if we put him in outside activities his attitude will improve.

122

Maybe if I leave his father, we'll all feel better." Many parents of ADD teens attribute their problems to outside forces and feel that making radical life-style changes will help. Without the right treatment, however, these changes are rarely helpful.

Depression -- "I'm a failure as a parent. I've failed my teenager. I have no business raising children. I should go to work and leave him with other people. I'm so tired that I can't do this anymore." The physical and emotional drain of having an ADD teen can often trigger off a significant depression.

Siblings

Teenagers with ADD often irritate their siblings to the point of causing tears, anger or fighting. Siblings develop negative feelings toward the ADD teen because they are often embarrassed by their outrageous behavior at school or with friends.

Since ADD, for the most part, is a genetic disorder, it is more likely that siblings may also have features of ADD. Having two or more members of a family with untreated ADD can completely disorganize the family.

Often times in families with an ADD child or teenager, there is an identified "good" child and a "bad" (ADD) child. Because the parents' self-esteem is so damaged by having an unrecognized ADD child they will often avoid the ADD child and focus a lot of positive energy on the other child. They might think that they are more "perfect" than they really are. This causes resentment in the ADD child or teen. It also causes the "perfect" child to sabotage the progress that the ADD teen might make. Here's an example:

Sally, age 14, has ADD. She frequently complained that her 12-year-old sister, Betts, would lie to get her in trouble. They shared a room together, and Betts often told their mother that Sally messed up the room when she hadn't. Since Sally was often already in trouble the mother always believed Betts and Sally was scolded by the mother.

Here are common feelings experienced by the brothers and sisters of siblings with ADD.

Embarrassment -- just as parents are blamed by neighbors for unacceptable behavior of their child, so brothers and sisters are often held responsible or ridiculed by their peers for the actions of their ADD sibling.

Anger -- an ADD child can evoke intense emotions in his brother or sister, often from the conflict seeking behavior.

Resentment -- a sibling may feel very resentful at all the fighting, tension and turmoil that goes on at home.

Guilt -- like parents, siblings often feel guilty for emotions they harbor. They care deeply in spite of the behavior they live with.

Lack of Control -- brothers and sisters find it difficult to be with the ADD teen without constant struggles over rules and issues of control. They may strike out at the ADD sibling as a result of being constantly frustrated.

Jealousy -- siblings often question the double standards that exist in the rules that they are governed by. The ADD teen is often rewarded when the behavior does not warrant it as a way of pacifying him or her at the time.

The ADD Teenager

Teenagers with ADD often feel alone and alienated from their families. The years of tension, turmoil and frustration often cause emotional distance. Many ADD teenagers want to leave home as soon as they can. Yet, when they try to leave home they discover that they don't have adequate skills or resources to make it work.

Often ADD teenagers feel blamed for every bad thing that happens in a family and they try to escape the bad feelings. The frustration may lead to drug abuse, running away or criminal behavior.

Healing Tips For Families With ADD

1. Get medical help. Teenagers or their families who deny that ADD is a problem only perpetuate the problems to go on and on.

2. Every member of the family who has ADD needs to be treated. Untreated family members can cause serious turmoil in the family.

3. Regularly take your medication. ADD is a medical disorder and medication is an important part of the treatment.

4. Watch the timing of the medication. If family turmoil seems to happen in the evenings or early in the morning adjust the timing of medication to cover those times.

5. Assume the best about your parents. They are probably trying to do the best they can given the circumstances of their lives. When you have a positive attitude it is likely to rub off on them.

6. Get into the habit of thinking of the consequences of what you say or do before you say or do it.

7. Forgive the people who have treated you unfairly because they didn't understand ADD. Harboring bad feelings has a negative effect on your mind and your body and it only hurts you. Understand that ADD has a negative impact on a family. Forgiveness and understanding go a long way in helping families heal.

8. Get rid of the guilt you feel. Guilt doesn't change behavior. Focus your thoughts in a positive way to help make your family a better place to live.

9. Be a good listener. Before you open your mouth to respond to someone repeat back what the other person said to make sure you really understand them.

10. Take an "emotional time out" when things are heating up. Tell the other person you need to take a break and that you'll continue the discussion in a few minutes.

11. When you find yourself ready to get angry take 5 deep breaths just to clear your mind and focus your thoughts.

12. Spend time asking yourself what kind of relationship you want with your family. Most teenagers we know want to have a kind, caring, loving relationship with their family. Ask yourself everyday if your behavior fits with the goals you have for your family.

13. Learn to recognize when you're stirring up trouble. A lot of ADD teens say they like to argue just to argue. Fight the tendency to fight.

14. Take responsibility to help the family make changes, rather than feel like you're a victim.

15. Have hope that things will change. As long as you have life and breath there is always hope.

Chapter 13:

A.D.D. and Friends

Initially, many people with ADD make wonderful friends. They are talkative, full of energy, have lots of ideas and are independent. After a while, however, making and keeping friends is difficult for many people with ADD. It is estimated that at least half of all children and teens with ADD have problems with their peers and up to 75% of adults have interpersonal problems. Here are several of the reasons for social problems:

There is a high rate of intrusive or disruptive behaviors (excessive talking, interrupting, noisy and obnoxious behavior, monopolizing discussions).

Problems taking turns and sharing, difficulty following others in conversations, poor eye contact and inappropriate verbal interchanges are also common.

Poor emotional control (excitability, moodiness, temper outbursts, overreaction to minor events) can also be a problem.

Impulsivity (saying or doing things that are thoughtless) often devastates a relationship and causes bad feelings between friends. This is one reason many people with ADD lose friendships. They say the first thing that comes into their heads without asking themselves whether or not it would be helpful to say. For example, when someone makes you mad, most of us think of things to say that hurt the other person. It's usually not helpful to say it, but rather to take some time before you respond. Darcy (ADD) had been friends with Penny for years. It was a stormy friendship. They had many things in common (sports and church), but Darcy would just say hurtful comments that would cause them to not speak to each other for weeks. One time Penny confided in Darcy about how upset she was that a particular guy had not asked her to the dance. Darcy said, "If you'd lose some of that weight maybe you'd be more appealing." Penny, already feeling bad, started to cry and didn't speak to Darcy for a month.

Distractibility (trouble focusing on others) often irritates others and can cause problems in friendships.

SRJ:

No one will go to the movies with me. During the movie I always get lost and ask others what's going on. They get frustrated and give me dirty looks.

A lack of follow through (making relationships feel one sided from the other person's point of view) can also cause hurt feelings.

Low self-esteem often causes teens with ADD to do things to "fit in." Ben, age 16, worked at a grocery store. He was diagnosed with ADD when he was 12. His friends liked to go to parties and drink. Ben wanted to be part of the group. He had problems fitting in with the other kids ever since he was in elementary school. At first, when his friends asked him to steal alcohol for them he said no. But feeling lonely, he decided to go ahead and do it. The first time he did it, nothing happened. The other kids paid more attention to him. He kept doing it. After the fourth time he stole alcohol for his friends he was caught. The parents who caught the kids drinking, demanded to know how they got the alcohol. His "friends" blamed Ben. Ben was arrested and was sent to juvenile hall for stealing.

Understanding how to be effective in friendships is very important to being a happy teenager (or adult for that matter). Here are some suggestions:

1. Explain ADD to your friends. Other people are often more understanding if they know that there's a problem.

2. If you need your medication to be thoughtful and less impulsive, take it when you're going to be around your friends.

3. Apologize when you say or do impulsive things that hurt someone else's feelings. Having the ability to "say you're sorry" is a good human trait.

4. Don't let others pressure you into doing things against your moral values (such as drugs, criminal behavior, or teasing other kids). When you do things to fit in, you end up hating yourself later on (you might also end up in juvenile hall).

5. Become a good listener. Repeat back what you hear from others before impulsively responding to them.

6. Hang out with other people who have the same goals you have. Who you spend time with really matters! If you spend time with teens who are doing well in school, you are likely to do well in school to fit into the group. It is part of the "culture" of the group. When you hang out with teens who do drugs or who don't care about school, you're more likely to do drugs or "blow off" school. You become like the people you hang out with.

7. Be trustworthy. Friends become closer when they know they can confide in each other. Sometimes the impulsivity associated with ADD causes people to accidentally betray their friendships. Watch your mouth!!

8. Be considerate. Think about ways to help out your friends when they need it.

9. Be flexible. Many teens with ADD are very stubborn. This does not help friendships. The goal of friendship is to share time together, not control the other person.

10. Don't take advantage of your friends! Make sure relationships are "give and take" and that there is a sense of equality and fairness. Many friends of people with ADD say that they have a tendency to be selfish. Treat others like you would like to be treated.

Chapter 14:

The Impact Of A.D.D. On Love Relationships

Love relationships are often seriously affected by ADD. Falling in love is an important part of making us human. It is necessary for our emotional health. Yet, it seems for many teenagers with ADD, falling and staying in love can pose real challenges. Here are some of the problems:

Distractibility:

Due to distractibility, conversations are often cut short or left un-completed, leaving the other person feeling unimportant. Many people who go out with teens who have ADD complain that they are often inattentive or look around at other people.

Teasing:

The person with ADD often teases others, sometimes to the point where the other person becomes very upset. Dr. Amen has one pa-tient who gave his wife a heart condition. He would hide around corners and jump out in front of her to scare her. She never knows what to expect.

Fighting:

Fighting is typical for many people with ADD. It may be related to impulsivity (saying things without thinking), stimulation-seeking behavior, misperceptions, rage outbursts and chronically low self-esteem. Chronic conflict is very common in ADD relationships. It is important to emphasize that the "conflict-seeking" behavior is unconscious. The person doesn't wake up in the morning thinking that they want to start a fight, yet they do it over and over and over.

Problems Taking Turns:

The ADD person's need to have what they want right away often causes problems in situations where they need to take turns, such as in conversations or games.

Speaking Without Thinking:

This is perhaps the most damaging problem with ADD in relationships. Just because a person has a thought doesn't mean that it is accurate or that they necessarily believe it. Many teens with ADD just say what comes to mind. They then get stuck in defending these statements, which causes further problems.

Easily Frustrated/Emotional/Moody

Many boyfriends and girlfriends of ADD teens tell us that they never know what to expect. "One minute she's happy, the next minute she's screaming," is a common complaint. Small amounts of stress may trigger off huge explosions.

Tantrums/Rage Outbursts

Some studies have reported that up to 85% of people with ADD have rage outbursts, often with little provocation. After this occurs several times in a relationship, the partner becomes "gun shy" and starts to withdraw from the person. Untreated ADD is often involved in abusive relationships.

Low Self-Esteem

When people do not feel good about themselves, it impairs their ability to relate to others. They have difficulty taking compliments or getting outside of themselves to truly understand the other person. The brain filters information coming in from the environment. When the brain's filter (self-esteem) is negative, people tend to only see the negative and ignore any positive. Many partners of ADD people complain that when they give their partner a compliment, they find a way to make it look like they have just been criticized.

Looking for Turmoil:

This is a common complaint of people living with someone who has ADD. They say that the person looks for trouble. Rather than ignoring a minor incident, he or she focuses on it and has difficulty letting it go. Things in an ADD relationship often do not remain peaceful for long periods of time.

Failure to See Others' Needs:

Many people with ADD have trouble getting outside of themselves to see the emotional needs of others. They are often labeled as spoiled, immature or self-centered.

10 Ways To Ruin A Good Relationship

Dr. A:

Here are 10 ways to ruin a good relationship. Do the opposite to have the best love relationships.

1. **Blame the other person**. Many people fail to take responsibility for their part in a relationship. Subsequently, they spend a lot of time blaming the other person for the relationships shortcomings. When this occurs, the relationship is doomed to unhappiness and possible death. Take responsibility for the relationship and look for what you can do to improve it, rather than waiting for the other person to take the initiative.

2. **Take the relationship for granted**. In order for relationships to be special they need constant nurturing. The relationship suffers when it gets put low on the priority list of time and attention. Focusing on what you want in a relationship is essential for making it happen.

3. **Discount the other person**. A sure fire way to doom a relationship is to discount, belittle or degrade the other person. Unfortunately, many people use these forms of negative control to have power in a relationship, but they don't understand how it erodes the foundation. Protect your relationships by building up the other person.

4. **Get into a rut**. When relationships become stale or boring they become vulnerable to erosion. A lack of interesting conversation or activity sets up people to look elsewhere to find excitement. Stay away from "the same old thing" by looking for new and different ways to add life to your relationships.

5. **Fail to notice the good**. It's very easy to notice what you do not like about a relationship. That's almost our nature. Most people notice ten times more negative things they don't like rather than the positive things about the relationship that they do like. It takes real effort to notice what you like. When you spend more time noticing the positive aspects of the relationship, you're more likely to see an increase in positive behavior.

6. **Miscommunication**. Not clearly understanding another person, jumping to conclusions or mind reading are ways to really hurt a good relationship. I'm convinced most of the fights people have stem from some form of miscommunication. Take time to really listen and clarify what other people say to you. Don't react to what you think someone means, ask them what they mean and then formulate a response.

7. **Violate trust**. So many relationships fall apart after there has been a major violation in trust, such as an affair or other forms of dishonesty. Often hurts in the present, even minor ones, remind us of major traumas in the past and we blow them way out of proportion. Once a violation of trust has occurred try to understand why it happened.

8. **Lack empathy**. Empathy is being able to understand things from another person's point of view. Many people lack the knowledge or desire to understand anything outside of themselves. This self-centeredness destroys the critical balance needed in order for closeness to occur. Putting yourself in the "other person's shoes" is crucial to healthy relationships.

9. **Avoid conflict, "people pleaser."** Whenever you give in to another person to avoid a fight you give away a little of your power.

If you do this over time you give away a lot of power and begin to resent the relationship. Avoiding conflict in the short run often has devastating long term effects. Stick up for what you know is right and it will be better for the relationship.

10. **A lack of time**. Sadly, time spent in important relationships are often the first thing to suffer in our busy life-styles. Relationships require real time in order to function. Many couples who both work and have children often find themselves growing further apart because they have no time together. When they do get time together they often realize how much they really do like each other. Make your special relationships a "time investment" and it will pay dividends for years to come.

Avoiding these ten common relational mistakes will help you feel good with the people you care about in your life.

A man can fail many times, but he isn't a failure until he begins to blame someone else.

John Burroughs

PART III.

EXCELLING WITH A.D.D.

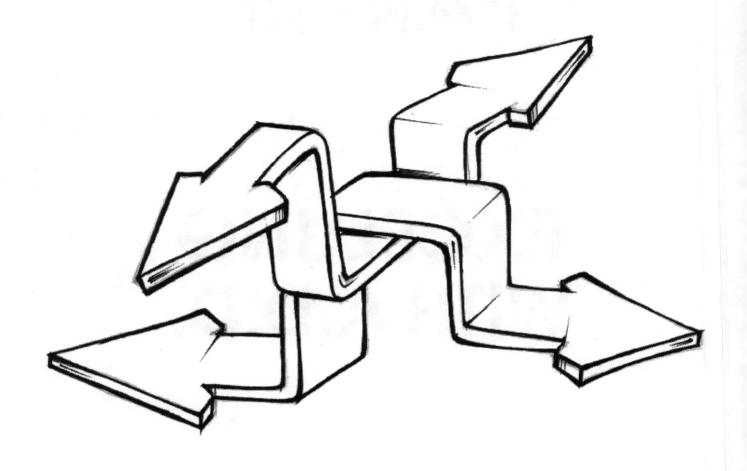

Where's your direction?

Chapter 15:

The Impact Of A.D.D. On Self-Esteem

By the age of 6 or 7, ADD often has a significant negative impact on self-esteem. Here are some of the reasons why:

Frequent Conflict:

For many, they have been in conflict with either their parents, friends or teachers over and over for years. This causes them to develop negative "self-talk" patterns and low self-esteem.

Negative Input:

The difficult behavior associated with ADD often incites negative input from others. "Don't do that. Why did you do that? Where was your head? What's wrong with you? Your brother doesn't act like that! You'd do better if you would try harder. Shame on you!" These are common phrases many ADD teens hear on a regular basis. Our brains work like a computer -- negative input turns into low self-esteem.

Inaccurate self-assessment:

As mentioned above, people with ADD are often a poor judge of their own ability. They often devalue their strengths and positive attributes, focusing only on their failures.

Chronic Failure:

Most people with ADD have had many failure experiences in life, school, relationships and work. These failures set them up to expect failure, and whenever a person expects that they will fail, they don't try their best or they don't try at all.

Negative Bonding

ADD often causes negative bonding with parents. Bonding is critical to the emotional health of human beings. Yet, by the time many ADD children are school age, they have such a negative relationship with their parents that they begin not to care about other people, which set them up for societal problems. Without bonding, people do not care about others, and when a person doesn't care, he or she has no problems hurting others to get what they want.

A Sense Of Being Damaged

Due to the many problems that ADD people have experienced throughout their lives, they often have a sense that they are different from others and that they are "damaged."

Tantrums/Rage Outbursts

There is a high incidence of rage outbursts, in people with ADD. Each outburst lowers the person's self esteem as they sense being out of control.

Brain Filters

When people do not feel good about themselves, it impairs their ability to relate to others. They have difficulty taking compliments or getting outside of themselves to truly understand the other person. The brain filters information coming in from the environment. When the brain's filter (self-esteem) is negative, people tend to only see the negative and ignore any positive.

Negative Thinking Patterns

Thought patterns are the manifestation of self-esteem. Due to difficult past life experiences, many people with ADD have a tendency to think very negatively. They frequently distort situations to make them out to be worse than they really are. They tend to mind read, overgeneralize, think in black or white terms, predict bad outcomes, label themselves with negative terms and personalize situations that have little meaning. Teaching the ADD person to talk back to negative thoughts is essential to helping them heal.

Chapter 16:

How To Stay Motivated

Staying motivated is often a major challenge for people with ADD. Often the level of failure and frustration has been so high throughout a person's life that they feel helpless or powerless to change their situations.

If you place a grasshopper in a jar with a lid, you can learn a powerful lesson about motivation. Grasshoppers in this kind of captivity behave as many people do throughout their lives.

At first, the imprisoned grasshoppers try desperately to escape from the jar, using their powerful hind legs to launch their bodies up against the lid. They try and try, and then they try again. Initially, they are very persistent. They may try to get out of their trap for several hours.

When they finally stop, however, their trying days are over. They will never again try to escape from the jar by jumping. You could take the lid off of the jar and have a pet grasshopper for life. Once they believe that they cannot change their situation, that's it. They stop trying.

In a similar way, once an elephant learns something, it stays with him for life. Many circus elephants are trained as babies to stay in one place by placing a strong chain around one ankle. Like the grasshoppers, they initially struggle and struggle to get free until they cannot struggle any more. Once they stop the struggling they will never again try to break loose from something holding them by the ankle. Powerful adult elephants can be held in place by just a thin rope around one of their legs. It has been reported that elephants have burned to death in circus fires when the huge beasts were tethered by small, easily broken ropes around their legs.

It is easy to see the parallel between grasshoppers and elephants, and people who get stuck in negative patterns of behavior: Once they believe they are defeated, that they cannot do things to change their situation, they stop trying--they give up, never to try again. Even if the lid is removed from their traps, it doesn't occur to them to leave; even if success or happiness is within their grasp, they are unable to reach out and grab it. They remain stuck in a no-go mode, in a habit of defeat, that stays with them until they die.

You are not a grasshopper. And you are not an elephant, or, for that matter, any other lower form of life. You are a human being, the highest form of life ever known. You are separated from these lower life forms by your ability to think, your ability to reason, and, most importantly, your ability to adapt and change as the environment dictates. Adaptability is the reason human beings, despite being smaller and weaker than many animal species, have come to rule the world.

Once you find out you have ADD it is important to evaluate the areas of your life where you feel stuck: relationships, work, health or spiritual life. Do you have the attitude of an imprisoned grasshopper from struggling with untreated ADD? Or do you actively seek to change the negative patterns in your life? Proper treatment for ADD is like taking the lid off of your situation, freeing you to change difficult patterns. But, rather than the grasshopper who has stopped trying, once you begin treatment it is essential to rethink your position and leave the comfort of the jar. Take the op portunities that are available to you, rather than stay stuck in the patterns of the past. You are not a grasshopper.

Here are some tips on avoiding grasshopper behavior and staying motivated:

1. Stay focused! Constantly keep your goals in mind. Write out clear goals for each of the major areas of your life: relationships, school, work, money, health and spirituality. Look at your goals everyday. Writing clear goals helps to keep you focused. A famous East Coast university recently had a twenty year class reunion. At graduation only 3% of the students had written, clearly defined goals for themselves. At the reunion, the 3% of the class with the clear sense of focus in their lives were worth more than the combined value of the 97% of people without goals. Learn early to set clear goals for yourself.

I have developed a simple "focus" exercise for children, teens and adults called the "One Page Miracle." On one piece of paper have the child write out their goals: in their relationships, at school, for their money and individually. Here are the categories of the "One Page Miracle" which I usually recommend:

RELATIONSHIPS (parents, siblings, friends, other family members, grandparents, aunts, etc.)

SCHOOL (knowledge, relationship with teacher, grades, working toward career goals, etc.)

MONEY (for current wants and needs, to save for future wants and needs)

SELF (body, mind, spirit, interests)

Here are several examples of the kind of statements that are helpful in the "One Page Miracle":

RELATIONSHIPS

Parents:
* to have good communication with them
* to ask for help and support when I need it
* to give love and support, especially when I see that they need it
* have a good relationship with them

Brothers/
Sisters:
* have a good relationship with them
* be kind to each other

Friends:
* get a long with my friends
* make new friends
* be able to do fun things together

SCHOOL
* learn the most I can from everyday, even when I don't feel like it
* do the best I can
* have most of my reports done three days before they are due

MONEY
* save some to buy the things I want
* have money to go to college

                    * be able to buy a car before I'm 18

SELF

Body: * be healthy and strong

Mind: * feel happy and be in good control of myself

Spirit: * pray everyday to keep close to God and keep myself
               on track toward doing what is right

Interests: * learn new things (such as how electricity works)

Doing the "One Page Miracle" every couple of months will be one of the best gifts you can give yourself.

Develop clear goals

2. Spend time with teenagers who are motivated and who want to do well. You become like the people with whom you hang out. If you spend a lot of time with kids who get into trouble, you're likely to get into trouble. If you spend time with teens who use drugs or get involved with premature sex, you're more likely to use drugs or become involved prematurely with sex. If you spend time with teens who care about school and who want to do well in school you're more likely to care about school and do well. Because of the level of trouble that has followed many teens with ADD they tend to hang out with others who get into trouble. This is very important to change if you want to stay motivated toward success in your life.

Hang out with people you want to be like

3. Work in steps, learn to be patient. Because impulsivity is a part of ADD, many ADD teens are impatient and want things to happen right away. Learn to delay what you want so that you can have better things down the road. It is estimated that you will make $100,000 more in your life for each year you attend college; If you get a four year degree you'll (on average) make $600,000 more in your life; and if you get an advanced degree, such as a doctor or attorney, you'll make an average of $2,200,000 more in your life. Learn to delay gratification of the moment for better things down the road.

Work in steps, be patient

4. Develop a library of positive experiences in your head. Your brain stores highly charged emotional memories. In order to stay motivated it is often helpful to activate as many positive memories as possible, especially the memories of the best times of your life, and the times you felt the most competent in your life. Many therapists have depressed people go back through all of the negative experiences in their lives, looking for keys to the depression. Unfortunately, this form of treatment is misguided. Depressed people have emotional filters that are set on "negative." The things they remember are negative, and remembering them only makes the depressed person feel worse.

To bring healing to your brain, it is important to remember the best times of your life. Times that were charged with positive emotions. Make a list of the 10 happiest times in your life. Describe those times in detail. Use as many of the five senses as possible (what the event looked like, smelled like, tasted like, felt like and sounded like). In a metaphorical sense, go to the library of experiences everyday. Focus and remember the best times in your life.

Counting your blessings can be very healing.

5. Predict the best. The expectation of success is a very powerful motivating force by itself. Many teens with ADD are experts at predicting the worst. Learning to overcome the tendency toward negative predictions is very helpful in motivation. Through the years, I have met many people with ADD who tell me that they're pessimists. They say that if they expect the worst to happen in a situation, they will never be disappointed. Even though they may never be disappointed, they are likely to die earlier. Your thoughts effect every cell in your body.

Physicians have known for centuries that positive expectations play a crucial role in the outcome of many illnesses. Until one hundred to one hundred and fifty years ago, the history of medical therapeutics was largely that of the doctor-patient relationship and the "placebo effect" (placebos being inert substances that have no physiological effect on the problem; also called sugar pills, or in Britain, dummy pills). Actually, most of the treatments by physicians back then would have been more harmful than beneficial to the patient. Four of the most famous medications used by physicians until about the eighteenth century were unicorn's horn, used to detect and protect against poisons in wines; benzoar stones, as antidotes for all kinds of poisons; theriac, a mixture of many drugs plus honey, as a universal antidote; and powdered Egyptian mummy, as a universal remedy for almost all ailments, including wound healing. (The unicorn's horn usually came from the ivory of the narwhal or the elephant.) Doctors were dangerous to patients. What is surprising, however, is that, in spite of the harmful treatments, many patients, in fact, improved or recovered completely.

The benefits of the placebo effect are determined by the expectations and hopes shared by the patient and the doctor. According to Dr. T. Findley, action, ritual, faith and enthusiasm are the important ingredients. Jerome Frank, M.D., after studying the psychotherapeutic process, concluded that the belief of the therapist in his treatment and the belief of the patient in the therapist were the most important factors in a positive outcome to therapy.

Believe the best.

6. Have meaning, purpose, stimulation and excitement in your life to prevent shutdown. Meaning, purpose, stimulation and excitement are very important in activating your motivation. As we have mentioned many of the symptoms of ADD differ under different circumstances. For routine, regular, mundane activities, people with ADD often have serious problems. However, when they are engaged in interesting, exciting, stimulating tasks, they often excel. A helpful tip is to make sure you go into a line of work you love. It can make all the difference between success and chronic failure.

Meaning, purpose and stimulation.

7. Abraham Lincoln built a lifetime of accomplishments out of defeats. Look at his record.

He lost his job in 1832.
He was defeated for the legislature in 1832.
He failed in business in 1833.
He was elected to the legislature in 1834.
His sweetheart died in 1835.

He had a nervous breakdown in 1836.
He was defeated for Speaker in 1838.
He was defeated for the nomination for Congress in 1843.
He was elected to Congress in 1846.
He lost the renomination in 1848.
He was rejected for land officer in 1849.
He was defeated for the Senate in 1854.
He was defeated for the nomination for Vice-President in 1856.
He, again, was defeated for the Senate in 1858.
He was elected President in 1860.

Failure is a part of everyone's life. No one starts out walking in life; it is months before we even learn how to crawl. It is not failure that holds people back, it is their attitude toward failure and their fear of it. Toddlers don't give up when they fall; they take their bruises and try again. Anyone who has had small children knows that despite many failed attempts at mobilization, most children go very quickly from crawling to walking to running to climbing up to places they shouldn't.

It is arrogant to think that we are perfect and we will never fail. We are not programmed with the answers, we learn them. We get the right answers by learning processes and observing our errors along the way. Successful supervisors do not get angry when their employees make mistakes. They say, "Don't be afraid to make mistakes; learn from them. Just don't make the same one twice. Observe what you do and you'll always improve."

How supervisors deal with the mistakes of their employees often determines the quality of the employees. When people go to work and they expect to be yelled at or belittled their fear and anger get in the way of them doing the best they can. When they go to work and know that they will be taught to learn from their mistakes in a positive atmosphere they relax and are more likely to produce good work.

Be a good teacher for yourself and those around you. Maturity is being able to learn from the mistakes you make in a positive atmosphere. The human brain is expert at learning. It is essential to give it every chance to learn, and not to expect it to know things it hasn't learned. The brain learns best in a positive, relaxed environment. Be kind to yourself. Learn from failures, don't beat yourself up for them.

Failure is not fatal. Not trying is!

Chapter 17:

Overcoming Negative Thinking Patterns Associated With A.D.D.

Due to the negativity and failure that many teens with ADD have experienced throughout their lives they often develop negative thinking patterns that hold them back from becoming successful. Here are several thoughts that can ruin how you feel.

"Nothing will ever work out for me."

"Everyone does better than I do."

"Anybody could have done that. I'm not so special."

"The teacher doesn't like me."

"The whole class will laugh at me."

"You don't care about me."

"It's my fault my parents are fighting."

"I'm stupid."

"It's the teacher's fault I'm failing."

These are examples of thoughts that severely limit a teenager's ability to enjoy his or her life. How you think "moment by moment" has a huge impact on how you feel and how you behave. Negative thoughts often drive difficult behaviors and they cause most of the internal "feeling" problems that teens have, as well as the external or social problems. Hopeful thoughts, on the other hand, influence positive behaviors and lead teenagers to feel good about themselves and be more effective in their day-to-day lives.

Most teenagers with ADD have a lot of negative thoughts. These thoughts come from many sources. Some of the negative thoughts come from what other people have told them about themselves (i.e., "You're no good! Why can't you ever mind? What's the matter with you. Why don't you pay attention!"). Other negative thoughts originate from experiences where the teen is continually frustrated, either at home or at school. They begin to think thoughts such as, "I'm stupid. I can't ever do anything right. It will never work out for me."

Your Brain Works Like A Computer

In many ways our brain works like a computer. When teens receive negative **input** about themselves, they **store** it in their subconscious mind and they then **express** those messages in their negative behavior or feelings. Unless teens are taught how to talk back to these harmful messages, they believe them 100%. This is a very important point. Most teens (and adults) never challenge the thoughts that go through their head. They never even think about their own thoughts. They just believe what they think, even though the thoughts may be very irrational. This leads to behavior that is based on false ideas or false assumptions.

Positive Programming Versus Negative Programming

Parents often program the thoughts of their children and teens by how they talk to them. In dealing with children and teens, it's important to program their mind with positive, uplifting, hopeful words, rather than critical or harsh words.

Many teens with ADD have trouble thinking logically (although this seems to be a common adult problem as well). Unfortunately, many teens carry these negative thought patterns into adulthood, causing them to have problems with their moods and behavior.

These negative thoughts affect their moods and in many teens become the seeds of anxiety or depression later on in life. It's critical to teach yourself about your thoughts and to learn how to challenge what you think, rather than just accepting thoughts blindly.

Thinking Skills

Unfortunately, when you're a child no one teaches you to think much about your thoughts or to challenge the notions that go through your head, even though your thoughts are always with you. Why do we spend so much time teaching kids about diagramming sentences and so little time teaching them how to think clearly? Most people do not understand how important thoughts are, and leave the development of thought patterns to random chance.

Did you know that thoughts have actual weight and mass? They are real! They have significant influence on every cell in your body (more detail on this in a little bit). When a teen's mind is burdened with many negative thoughts, it affects their ability to learn, their ability to relate to other people and their physical health. Teaching yourself how to control and direct your thoughts in a positive way will be one of the greatest gifts you can give yourself.

Here are the actual step-by-step "positive thinking" principles that Dr. Amen uses in his psychotherapy practice with children and teenagers. If you learn these principles, you will gain more control over your feelings and behavior.

STEP #1

Did you know...Every time you have a thought your brain releases chemicals. That's how our brains work.

you have a thought,

your brain releases chemicals,

an electrical transmission goes across your brain and

you become aware of what you're thinking.

Thoughts are real and they have a real impact on how you feel and how you behave.

STEP #2

Every time you have a mad thought, an unkind thought, a sad thought, or a cranky thought, your brain releases negative chemicals that make your body feel bad. Whenever you're upset, imagine that your brain releases bubbles with sad or angry faces,

157

looking to cause problems. Think about the last time you were mad. What did you feel inside your body? When most teens are mad, their muscles get tense, their heart beats faster, their hands start to sweat and they may even begin to feel a little dizzy. Your body reacts to every negative thought you have.

STEP #3

Every time you have a good thought, a happy thought, a hopeful thought or a kind thought your brain releases chemicals that make your body feel good. Whenever you're happy, imagine that your brain releases bubbles with glad or smiling faces, making you feel good. Think about the last time you had a really happy thought (such as when you got a good grade on a test or played with your pet). What did you feel inside your body? When most teens are happy, their muscles relax, their heart beats slower, their hands become dry and they breathe slower. Your body also reacts to your good thoughts.

STEP #4

Your body reacts to every thought you have. We know this from polygraphs or lie detector tests. During a lie detector test, you are hooked up to some very fancy equipment which measures:

hand temperature,
heart rate,
blood pressure,
breathing rate,
muscle tension and
how much the hands sweat.

The tester then asks you questions, like "Did you do that thing?" If you did the bad thing, your body is likely to have a **"stress response"** and it is likely to react in the following ways:

hands get colder,
heart goes faster,
blood pressure goes up,
breathing gets faster,
muscles get tight and
hands sweat more.

Almost immediately, your body reacts to what you think, whether you say anything or not. Now the opposite is also true. If you did not do the thing they are asking you about it is likely that your body will experience a **"relaxation response"** and react in the following ways:

hands will become warmer,
heart rate will slow,
blood pressure goes down,
breathing becomes slower and deeper,
muscles become more relaxed and
hands become drier.

Again, almost immediately, your body reacts to what you think. This not only happens when you're asked about telling the truth, your body reacts to every thought you have, whether it is about school, friends, family or anything else.

STEP #5

Thoughts are very powerful. They can make your mind and your body feel good or they can make you feel bad. Every cell in your body is affected by every thought you have. That is why when people get emotionally upset, they actually develop physical symptoms, such as headaches or stomach aches. Some people even think that people who have a lot of negative thoughts are more likely to get cancer. If you can think about good things you will feel better.

Did you know that Abraham Lincoln (our 16th president) had periods of bad depression when he was a child and later as an adult? He even thought about killing himself and had some days when he didn't even get out of bed. In his later life, however, he learned to treat his bad feelings with laughter. He became a very good storyteller and loved to tell jokes. He learned that when he laughed, he felt better. Over a hundred years ago, people knew that thoughts were very important!

STEP #6

Unless you think about your thoughts, they are **automatic or "they just happen."** Since they just happen, they are not always correct. Your thoughts do not always tell you the truth. Sometimes they even lie to you. Dr. Amen once knew a boy who thought he was stupid because he didn't do well on tests. When we tested his IQ (intelligence level), however, he discovered that he was close to a genius! You don't have to believe every thought that goes through your head. It's important to think about your thoughts to see if they help you or they hurt you. Unfortunately, if you never challenge your thoughts, you just "believe them" as if they were true.

STEP #7

You can train your thoughts to be positive and hopeful or you can just allow them to be negative and upset you. Once you learn about your thoughts you can choose to think good thoughts and feel good or you can choose to think bad thoughts and feel lousy. That's right, it's up to you! You can learn how to change your thoughts and you can learn to change the way you feel.

One way to learn how to change your thoughts is to notice them when they are negative and talk back to them. If you can correct negative thoughts you take away their power over you. When you just think a negative thought without challenging it, your mind believes it and your body reacts to it.

STEP #8

As we mentioned above, negative thoughts are mostly automatic or they "just happen." Dr. Amen calls these bad thoughts "**A**utomatic **N**egative **T**houghts." If you take the first letter from each of these words it spells the word **ANT**. Think of these negative thoughts that invade your mind like ants that bother people at a picnic. One negative thought, like one ant at a picnic, is not a big problem. Two or three negative thoughts, like two or three ants at a picnic, becomes more irritating. Ten or twenty negative thoughts, like ten or twenty ants at a picnic, can cause real problems.

Whenever you notice these automatic negative thoughts or ANTs, you need to crush them or they'll begin to ruin your whole day. One way to crush these ANTs is to write down the negative thought and talk back to it. For example, if you think, "Other teens will laugh at me when I give my speech" write it down and then write down a positive response; something like "The other teens will like my speech and find it interesting." When you write down negative thoughts and talk back to them, you take away their power and help yourself feel better.

Some teens have trouble talking back to these negative thoughts because they feel that they are lying to themselves. Initially, they believe that the thoughts that go through their mind are the truth. Remember, thoughts sometimes lie to you. It's important to check them out before you just believe them!

ANTs: Automatic Negative Thoughts

Here are nine different ways that our thoughts lie to us to make situations out to be worse than they really are. Think of these nine ways as different species or types of ANTs (automatic negative thoughts). When you can identify the type of ANT, you begin to take away the power it has over you. I have labeled some of these ANTs as red, because these ANTs are particularly harmful to you. Notice and exterminate ANTs whenever possible.

ANT SPECIES #1

All or nothing thinking:

These thoughts happen when you make something out to be all good or all bad. There's nothing in between. You see everything in black or white terms. The thought, "There's nothing to do," is an example of this. When you say "There's nothing to do" you feel down and upset. You feel bored and unmotivated to change the situation. You just whine or complain. But is, "There's nothing to do" a rational thought? Of course not, it's just a thought. Even on a day when it's raining outside and you have to stay in, you can probably list 20 things to do if you put your mind to it: draw, make paper airplanes, write a story, read a story, do a puzzle, write grandma a letter, do your chores (a novel thought), etc. But if you never challenge the thought, "There's nothing to do," then you just believe it and spend the rest of the day feeling crummy. Other examples of "all or nothing thinking" for teens include thoughts such as, "I'm the worst ballplayer in the city. If I get an A on this test I'm a great student, but if I do poorly then I'm no good at all."

ANT SPECIES #2

"Always" thinking:

This happens when you think something that happened will "always" repeat itself. For example, if your mother is irritable and she gets upset you might think to yourself, "She's **always** yelling at me." Even though she yells only once in a while. But just the thought "She's always yelling at me" is so negative that it makes you feel sad and upset. When ever you think in words like **always, never, no one, every one, every time, everything**, those are examples of "always" thinking and usually wrong. There are many examples of "always" thinking: "They always get to do everything, and I don't get to do anything. Every one is always picking on me. You never take me swimming. You always get her what she wants." This type of ANT is very common. Watch out for it.

ANT SPECIES #3 (red ANT)

Focusing on the negative:

This occurs when your thoughts **only see the bad in a situation** and ignore any of the good parts that might happen. For example, if you have to move, even though you're sad to leave your friends, you don't think of the new places you'll see and the new friends you'll make. It's very important, if you want to keep your mind healthy, to focus on the good parts of your life a lot more than the bad parts.

I once helped a child who was depressed. In the beginning he could only think about the bad things that happened to him. He had recently moved to my city and he told me that me that he would never have friends (even though he already had several), he would do poorly in his new school (even though he got mostly good grades) and that he would never have any fun (even though he lived near a bay and an amusement park). By focusing on the negative in his new situation, he was making it very hard on himself to adjust to his new home. He would have been much better off if he looked at all the positives in the situation rather than the negatives.

Negative people can learn a powerful lesson from the Disney movie "Pollyanna." In the movie, Pollyanna comes to live with her aunt after her missionary parents had died. Even though she had lost her parents, she was able to help many "negative people" with her attitude. She introduced them to the "glad game," to look for things to be glad about in any situation. Her father had taught her this game after she had experienced a disappointment. She had always wanted a doll, but her parents never had enough money to buy it for her. Her father sent a request for a secondhand doll to his missionary sponsors. By mistake, they sent her a pair of crutches. "What is there to be glad about crutches?" they thought. Then they decided they could be glad because they didn't have to use them. This very simple game changed the attitudes and lives of many people in the movie. The minister was especially affected by Pollyanna.

Before she came to town, he preached hell, fire and damnation, but he did not seem to be very happy. Pollyanna told him that her father said that the Bible had 800 "Glad Passages," and that if God mentioned being glad that many times, it must be because He wants us to think that way. Focusing on the negative in situations will make you feel bad. Playing the glad game, or looking for the positive, will help you feel better.

ANT SPECIES #4 (red ANT)

Fortune telling:

This is where you **predict the worst possible outcome** to a situation. For example, before you have to give a speech in front of the class you might say to yourself, "Other kids will laugh at me and think I'm stupid." Just having this thought will make you feel nervous and upset. I call "fortune telling" red ANTs because they really hurt your chances for feeling good.

Dr. Amen once treated a 10-year-old boy, named Kevin, who stuttered in class whenever he read out loud. In private, he was a wonderful reader, but whenever he started to read in class he thought to himself "I'm a lousy reader; the other kids will laugh at me." Because he had these thoughts, he stopped raising his hand to volunteer to read. In fact, this thought made him so upset that he started getting sick before school and missed nearly a month of school before his mother brought him to see me. He also stopped answering the telephone at home for fear that he would stutter whenever he said hello. When he told me about his thoughts in class and at home, I understood the problem. When you predict that bad things will happen, such as you will stutter, your mind then often makes them happen. For this child, when he saw himself stuttering in his mind, he then stuttered whenever he read in class.

The treatment for Kevin was to get him to replace those negative thoughts and pictures in his head with the image of him being a wonderful reader in class. I also taught him to breathe slowly when he read and to think good thoughts. I also made him the designated person to answer the telephone at home. Whenever you're afraid of unreasonable things (such as answering the telephone or reading in class), it is important to face your fears. Otherwise, fears develop power over you. Over the next couple of weeks he was able to go back to school, and he even volunteered to read. At home, his mother told me that he ran to answer the telephone whenever it rang. If you are going to predict anything at all, it is best to predict the best. It will help you feel good and it will help your mind to make it happen.

ANT SPECIES #5 (red ANT)

Mind reading:

This happens when you believe that you know what another person is thinking when they haven't even told you. Many people do mind reading, and more often than not it gets them into trouble. It is the major reason why teens have trouble in relationships with their friends. I tell teens, "Please don't read anybody's mind; they have enough trouble reading it themselves!" You know that you are doing mind reading when you have thoughts such as, "Those people are mad at me. You don't like me. They were talking about me."

I once treated a teenager, Dave, who had this problem so badly that he would hide in clothes racks at the shopping mall so that other kids wouldn't see him. He told me, "If they see me, they'll think I look funny and then they'll want to tease me." He became very nervous around other people because he worried about what others thought of him. He finally realized that other teenagers were more worried about themselves and they really spent little time thinking about him. Avoid reading anyone's mind. You never know what they are thinking.

ANT SPECIES #6

Thinking with your feelings:

This occurs when you believe your negative feelings without ever questioning them. Feelings are very complex, and, as I mentioned above, feelings sometimes lie to you. But many people believe their feelings even though they have no evidence for them. "Thinking with your feelings" thoughts usually start with the words "I feel." For example, "I feel like you don't love me. I feel stupid. I feel like a failure. I feel nobody will ever trust me." Whenever you have a strong negative feeling, check it out. Look for the evidence behind the feeling. Do you have real reasons to feel that way? Or, are your feelings based on events or things from the past?

Here's an example. Wesley, age 16, had a problem learning. He also got expelled from his school for fighting. He felt that he was stupid and that he was a bad person. When Dr. Amen first met him he diagnosed him with Attention Deficit Disorder. He started the

167

medicine and also went to a new school. He did wonderful! He did so well, in fact, that his old school (which was a better school) was willing to take him back. When his mother told him this good news, he became very upset. He said that he felt that he would fail and have lots of problems. He was letting the "old" feelings from the past mess up his chances for a new start. When he corrected his negative feelings by talking back to them, he was able to return to his old school. He even made the honor roll!

ANT SPECIES #7

Guilt beatings:

Guilt is not a helpful emotion, even for teens. In fact, guilt often causes you to do those things that you don't want to do. Guilt beatings happen when you think in words like "should, must, ought or have to." Here are some examples: "I should be nice to my younger brother. I must never lie. I ought to call my grandmother. I have to do my homework." Because of human nature, whenever we think that we "must" do something, no matter what it is, we don't want to do it.

Remember the story of Adam and Eve. The only restriction that God put on them when he gave them the Garden of Eden was that they shouldn't eat from the Tree of Knowledge. Almost immediately after God told them what they "shouldn't do" they started to wonder why they shouldn't do it. Well, you know the rest of the story. They ate from the tree and ended up being kicked out of the Garden of Eden . It is better to replace "guilt beatings" with phrases like "I want to do this...It fits my goals to do that...It would be helpful to do this.... So in our examples above, it would be helpful to change those phrases to "I want to be nice to my younger brother. It's helpful for me not to lie, because people will trust me. I want to call my grandmother. It's in my best interest to do my homework."

ANT SPECIES #8

Labeling:

Whenever you attach a negative label to yourself or to someone else, you stop your ability to take a clear look at the situation. Some examples of negative labels that teens use are "nerd," "jerk," "idiot," "loser" and "clown." Negative labels are very harmful, because whenever you call yourself or someone else a loser or an idiot you lump that person in your mind with all of the "losers" or "idiots" that you've ever known and you become unable to deal with them in a reasonable way. Stay away from negative labels.

ANT SPECIES #9
(the most poisonous red ANT)

Blame:

Teens who ruin their own lives have a strong tendency to blame other people when things go wrong in their life. They take little responsibility for their problems. When something goes wrong at home or at school, they try to find someone to blame. They rarely admit their own problems. Typically, you'll hear statements from them like:

"It wasn't my fault that...."

"That wouldn't have happened if you had...."

"How was I supposed to know...."

"It's your fault that...."

The bottom line statement goes something like this: "If only you had done something differently then I wouldn't be in the predicament I'm in. It's your fault, and I'm not responsible."

AJA:

Blaming others starts early. When my youngest sister, Katie, was 18 months old, she would blame me for any trouble she might be in. Her nickname for me was DiDi, and "Didi did it," even if I wasn't home. One day she spilled a drink at the table while my mother's back was turned. When mom turned around and saw the mess and asked her what had happened, Katie told her that "Didi spilled my drink." When mom told her that I was at a friend's house, Katie continued to say I did it. She said, "Didi came home, spilled my milk and then he left."

Whenever you blame someone else for the problems in your life you become powerless to change anything. Many teens (and adults) play the "Blame Game," but it rarely helps them. Stay away from blaming thoughts and take personal responsibility to change the problems you have.

SUMMARY OF ANT SPECIES:
(Automatic Negative Thoughts)

1. **All or nothing thinking**: thoughts that are all good or all bad.

2. **"Always" thinking**: thinking in words like always, never, no one, every one, every time, everything.

3. **Focusing on the negative**: only seeing the bad in a situation.

4. **Fortune telling**: predicting the worst possible outcome to a situation.

5. **Mind reading**: believing that you know what another person is thinking even though they haven't told you.

6. **Thinking with your feelings**: believing negative feelings without ever questioning them.

7. **Guilt beatings**: thinking in words like "should, must, ought or have to."

8. **Labeling**: attaching a negative label to yourself or others.

9. **Blame**: blaming someone else for the problems you have.

James Hammock

Rid yourself of the A.N.T.s in your life.

KILLING THE ANTs
(Talking Back To Negative Thoughts)

Whenever you notice an ANT entering your mind, train yourself to crush it. In a sense you become an exterminator of bad thoughts. To do this, write down the automatic negative thoughts (ANTs) that go through your mind. Then identify their species (such as "always thinking" or "mind reading"). Finally, kill the ANT by talking back to the irrational thought. When you do this exercise, you begin to take away the power of the ANTs and gain control over how you feel. Here are several examples from some of the bad thoughts at the beginning of the book.

Here are several examples of negative thoughts and ways to talk back to them and get them out of your head.

ANT	Species	Kill the A.N.T. (Talk Back)
I'll never be any good at math.	All or Nothing Thinking	Perhaps I'm not a math wizard, but with good help I can learn what I need.
No one will ever go out with me.	Always Thinking	That's silly. Lots of people will go out with me if I'm patient and thoughtful, and I ask them.
The teacher doesn't like me.	Mind Reading	I don't know that. Maybe she's just having a bad day.
The whole class will think my speech is stupid.	Fortune Telling	If I prepare and do a good job the class will like my speech. They are probably hoping I'll do a good job.

ANT	Species	Kill the A.N.T. (Talk Back)
This situation is not going to work out. I know something bad will happen.	Fortune Telling	Unless I have evidence that something bad will happen, I won't jump to conclusions. I'll be thoughtful and protect myself, but worrying is not going to help.
I'm stupid.	Labeling	Sometimes I do things that aren't that smart, but I'm not stupid!
It's your fault.	Blame	I need to look at my part of the problem and ways I can make the situation better.

Your thoughts matter! Train them to be positive and it will help your mind, your body and your relationships.

KILLING THE ANT EXERCISE
(Or Gaining Control Of Your Mind)

KILLING THE ANT exercise is for whenever you need to be in control of your mind. It is for times when you feel anxious, nervous, depressed or frazzled. It is for times when you need to be your best.

EVENT: Write out the event that is associated with your thoughts and feelings.

_____
_____
_____
_____

A.N.T.	**SPECIES**	**KILL THE A.N.T.**
(write out the automatic negative thoughts)	(identify the type of irrational thought)	(talk back to the irrational thoughts)

Notes:

Summary of ANT Types:

1. **All or nothing thinking:** all good or all bad.

2. **"Always" thinking:** always, never, every time, etc.

3. **Focusing on the negative:** only seeing the bad

4. **Fortune telling:** predicting the worst outcome

5. **Mind reading:** believing you know what others think
    The 18/40/60 Rule

6. **Thinking with your feelings:**
    believing negative feelings without questioning them.

7. **Guilt beatings:** "should, must, ought or have to."

8. **Labeling:** attaching a negative label to self or others.

9. **Blame:** blaming someone else for your problems.

Chapter 18

A.D.D. and Controlling Anger

Some researchers say that up to 85% of people with ADD have rage or anger attacks. If this applies to you it is essential to learn how to have better control over your temper. Anger can destroy relationships between friends, between a parent and a teen, and it can affect intimate relationships and work relationships. Here is a five part "Anger Management Plan."

One: Focus is essential. Before you do or say anything, ask yourself if your intended behavior fits with the goals you have for your life. For example, if you get angry at your sister or brother and think of telling him or her off, ask yourself if that behavior is going to help you have a kind, caring, loving, supportive relationship (which is probably your goal). Thinking before you act is critical to managing anger.

Two: Correct negative thoughts. As mentioned above, negative thought patterns can cause anger, depression and disappointment. Whenever you feel anger well up inside of you, write down the thoughts that drive your feelings. Odds are, they are a little irrational. Correcting them will give you more control of the situation.

Three: Get away from the situation until you calm down. Distraction is often very helpful in defusing angry situations. Write out "TEN THINGS TO DO WHEN I GET MAD" and keep the list where you can see it when the need arises. Here is a sample list from a sixteen-year-old. Adapt it for your own needs.

1. Listen to music.
2. Hit my punching bag.
3. Play a video game.
4. Go to my bedroom and read a book.
5. Work on homework.
6. Go for a walk.
7. Water the plants.
8. Watch TV.
9. Go to the garage and work with my tools.
10. Write about what I'm thinking and show it to a friend.

Four: Breathe slowly and deeply, mostly with your belly. The purpose of breathing is to get oxygen from the air into your body and to blow off waste products such as carbon dioxide. Every cell in your body needs oxygen in order to function. Brain cells are particularly sensitive to oxygen, as they start to die within four minutes when they are deprived of oxygen. Slight changes in oxygen content in the brain can alter the way a person feels and behaves. When a person gets angry, his or her breathing pattern changes almost immediately. Their breathing becomes more shallow and the rate increases significantly. This breathing pattern is inefficient and the oxygen content in the angry person's blood is lowered. Subsequently, there is less oxygen available to a person's brain and they may become more irritable, impulsive and confused, causing them to make bad decisions (such as to yell, threaten or hit another person).

Chapter 19:

Explaining A.D.D. To Others

Successfully dealing with ADD often means explaining it to other people, such as family members, friends, boyfriends, girlfriends, employers, and coaches. Certainly it is your choice on when and to whom you reveal this information. It is probably not smart to tell everyone you meet about your ADD; while at the same time, some people need to know and they will be in a position to make your life easier if they have accurate information about ADD. To help you think through the decision here are arguments both for and against telling others about your ADD.

Reasons to tell others:

-- need help or accommodations at school or work
-- help others understand certain behaviors you have
-- give others information about the medication you take
-- give others that may have the same or similar problem
   information that may be helpful for them

Reasons not to tell others:

-- no help or accommodations needed
-- lack of trust in how the person might use the information
-- may prejudice your position with the other person (such as an
   employer during an initial interview)

How to tell others about ADD

Taking the time to think through an explanation about ADD will help you relate this information to others in a clear way. How much you tell people about ADD depends on their need to know. Some people, such as family members and boyfriends or girlfriends need to know a lot; others, such as acquaintances or teammates may only need to know a little.

We'll give two sample "scripts" on how to explain ADD. One will be a simpler version. The other has more detail. Use these as guidelines.

A Brief Explanation of ADD

"My doctor has diagnosed me with ADD, which stands for attention deficit disorder. ADD is a condition where a person has trouble with concentration, attention span, organization, restlessness, and impulsivity. It is generally thought of as a problem that is present throughout a person's life and it tends to run in families.

Many recent studies suggest that ADD is a problem of how the brain functions. For most people, when they try to concentrate they get increased blood flow to the front part of the brain. This helps to keep them on track. For people with ADD, when they try to concentrate, blood flow in the front part of their brain actually decreases in activity (frontal lobe shutdown). Thus, the harder people with ADD try to concentrate, the worse things get.

Since ADD is a medical or physical problem doctors often use medication to treat some of the symptoms of ADD. Medications like Ritalin or Dexedrine, which are stimulants (strong forms of caffeine), stimulate the brain and prevent the frontal lobes from shutting down so that people with ADD can concentrate and have better follow through on tasks.

Many people with ADD are very smart and they come from all walks of life: doctors, lawyers, entertainers, accountants, plumbers, etc. Intelligence has nothing to do with ADD. Many people, despite being very smart, can have ADD which impairs their ability to live up to their potential. When left untreated, ADD can have a negative impact on all aspects of a person's life."

A Detailed Explanation of ADD

"My doctor has diagnosed me with ADD, which stands for attention deficit disorder. ADD is a condition where a person has trouble with concentration, attention span, organization, restlessness, and impulsivity. It is generally thought of as a problem that is present throughout a person's life and it tends to run in families.

Many recent studies suggest that ADD is a problem of how the brain functions. For most people, when they try to concentrate they get increased blood flow to the front part of the brain. This helps to keep them on track. For people with ADD, when they try to concentrate, blood flow in the front part of their brain actually decreases in activity (frontal lobe shutdown). Thus, the harder people with ADD try to concentrate, the worse things get.

Dr. Amen often uses the following analogy with his patients to explain ADD. 'ADD can be likened to driving a car. When most people put their foot on the gas pedal the car goes faster. For people with ADD, due to the frontal lobe shutdown, when they put their foot on the gas pedal their car goes slower (the harder they try the worse it gets).'

Comparing ADD to needing glasses is another helpful analogy Dr. Amen uses with his patients. He says, 'When a person needs glasses it is not their fault. They didn't do anything to cause the problem. Their eyeball has a funny shape which prevents them from seeing clearly. They are not crazy, or willful because they can't see clearly. Their mother didn't cause the problem with poor parenting skills. They just can't see clearly. Without glasses a person becomes ineffective and their life is much harder than it needs to be. In a similar way, when a person has ADD it is not their fault. ADD is a biological disorder, probably in the frontal lobes of the brain, that causes a person to have problems with focus and follow through. It's not their fault. Their mother didn't cause it. And without proper treatment, their lives will be much harder.'

Because of this frontal lobe shutdown many people with ADD can be 'stimulation seeking' as a way to keep themselves turned-on. They may unknowingly start arguments, get other people mad at them, or engage in risky behavior for the 'charge of the moment.' It is generally best to deal with someone who has ADD in a calm, soft, logical tone. Otherwise you might get sucked into a conflict.

Since ADD is a medical or physical problem doctors often use medication to treat some of the symptoms of ADD. Medications like Ritalin or Dexedrine, which are stimulants (strong forms of caffeine), stimulate the brain and prevent the frontal lobe shut down so that people with ADD can concentrate and have better follow through on tasks.

In addition to medication, there are other important parts to the treatment of ADD. Help with communication skills, organization, impulse control and self esteem are often needed. There are also several support groups for people with ADD. Education on ADD

often has a positive effect for the person with ADD and those who have contact with him or her.

Sometimes the treatment for ADD by itself is not enough. Accommodations, either at school or work, may be needed. Federal law considers ADD a 'handicapping condition,' and mandates that schools and employers provide environmental changes or accommodations to help the person with ADD be successful in their environment. Even though you can't 'see' ADD, it is just as real a disability as someone who has diabetes or a missing leg. Often the accommodations are simple and inexpensive, such as allowing students to type reports instead of writing them, giving them extra time on tests and frequently checking on their organization. At work, accommodations might include giving only one task at a time, providing an area free from distractions, closer supervision and help with organization of space and time.

Many people with ADD are very smart and they come from all walks of life: doctors, lawyers, entertainers, accountants, plumbers, etc. Intelligence has nothing to do with ADD. Many people, despite being very smart, can have ADD which impairs their ability to live up to their potential. When left untreated, ADD can have a negative impact on all aspects of a person's life."

You can add more details from the information you've learned from this book or other sources.

Chapter 20:

Understanding Medications For A.D.D.

Medication is most often an essential component to effective treatment for the ADD teen. As we've said many times now, ADD is a neurobiological disorder and needs to be treated as such. Without the right medication, the other interventions are often very ineffective. During Dr. Amen's child psychiatry training, his supervisors taught him to do play therapy with ADD children. It didn't work and he didn't much like these kids. Who likes playing war, hour after hour, and listening to parents complain that the child isn't getting any better? When these children are placed on the right medication, however, they can make very good use of their time in psychotherapy.

The goals of medication are to:

-- increase attention span and learning

-- decrease distractibility

-- decrease restlessness or high activity levels

-- decrease impulsiveness and increase thoughtfulness

-- decrease irritability

-- increase motivation

-- overall, improve functioning at school, at home, in relationships and with the self.

In Dr. Amen's experience, there are generally 4 classes of medication found to be effective in ADD, depending on the subtypes discussed above.

1. Stimulants:

methylphenidate (Ritalin)
dextroamphetamine (Dexedrine)
methamphetamine (Desoxyn)
magnesium pemoline (Cylert)
mixture of amphetamine salts (Adderall)

** contrary to popular belief, these are very safe medications
** with Cylert it is very important to monitor liver function tests, as 2-3% of people taking this medication may develop a chemical hepatitis

2. Tricyclic Antidepressants: (TCAs)

desipramine (Norpramin)
imipramine (Tofranil)
amitriptyline (Elavil)
nortryptiline (Pamelor)
clomipramine (Anafranil)

** these need to be monitored more closely than stimulants, especially their effect on heart function

** many teens respond to very low doses of these medications for ADD symptoms. This is important because the low doses often produce much fewer side effects than the higher "antidepressant" doses.

3. Antiobsessive or "anti-stuck" medications:

> fluoxetine (Prozac)
> clomipramine (Anafranil)
> (both a TCA and an anti-stuck medicine)
> sertraline (Zoloft)
> paroxetine (Paxil)
> fluvoxamine (Luvox)
> venlafaxine (Effexor)

** contrary to the negative media attention, Prozac, and medications like Prozac, are generally very safe and have few side effects. In a very small percentage of patients these medications may cause irritability or anxiety, but that is true with all antidepressants. If there are side effects on any medication, it is important to contact your doctor and discuss it.

4. Anticonvulsants or antiseizure medications:

> carbamazepine (Tegretol)
> valproic acid (Depakene or Depakote)
> gabapentin (Neurontin)

** it is important with these medications to watch the white blood cell counts and liver functions

** these are often helpful for people with ADD and violent out-bursts or those who have experienced a head trauma. Sometimes, a combination of medications is needed to obtain the full therapeutic effect. Dr. Amen particularly likes the combination of stimulants and anti-obsessive medications for children of alcoholics.

**The goal needs to be your best functioning,
not to be off medication!!**

The side effects of having ADD that is left untreated are immeasurably worse that those caused by the medication!!!

Common Questions
On The Use Of Stimulant Medications
for Attention Deficit Disorder

Stimulant medications include:

Ritalin (methylphenidate),
Dexedrine (dextroamphetamine),
Desoxyn (methamphetamine) and
Cylert (pemoline)
Adderall (mixture of amphetamine salts)

1. What Are The Uses For Stimulant Medications?

Stimulant medications have several uses in medicine. Most commonly, they are prescribed for ADD (both with and without hyperactivity). They are also used for narcolepsy (sudden sleep attacks), as an additional treatment for depression and to help thinking problems in the elderly.

2. How Can Stimulant Medications Help?

They can improve attention span, decrease distractibility, increase ability to finish tasks, improve ability to follow directions, decrease hyperactivity and restlessness and lessen impulsivity. Handwriting often improves with this medication. School work, homework and overall work performance often improve significantly. Aggression and stubbornness is often lessened. Improved listening and communication skills often occur, along with a decrease in stimulation or conflict seeking behaviors.

3. How Long Does The Medication Last? What Is The Usual Dosage?

Ritalin and Dexedrine usually last 3 to 4 hours, but in some people they last as little as 2 1/2 hours or as long as 6 hours. There is a slow release form of Ritalin that lasts 6-8 hours and may help you avoid taking a late morning or noon time dose. The slow release form of Ritalin has a reputation for being somewhat erratic. For some people it works great, for others not so good. Often you just have to try it to see. The slow release form of Dexedrine seems to be somewhat more reliable.

Dr. Amen usually prescribes medication for his patients in the afternoon and on weekends. During those times people with ADD still need to do work, homework or housework and interact with other people.

Everyone is different in their need for medication. Some people need small doses (2 1/2 to 5 milligrams) of stimulant medication twice a day, some need it four or five times a day (this is where antidepressants have some advantage over the stimulants, most of them are only given once a day).   Others need larger doses of stimulants (15 to 20 milligrams), response often does not necessarily correlate with body weight. Trial, supervision and observation are the keys to finding the right dose.

4. How Will The Doctor Monitor The Medication?

Most doctors see patients every couple of weeks until the right medication and dosage is found. During appointments doctors ask about progress (at home, school and work) and check for any side effects of the medication. A check on weight and height and occasionally blood pressure is common. When Cylert is used, it is critical to check blood work for liver function before starting and every couple of months thereafter. In addition, many doctors ask teachers to fill out follow-up rating scales to see the effectiveness of the medication. For adults, Dr. Amen asks that their spouses come to the appointments so that he can get another opinion on the patient's progress. He also asks for a teenager's parent and girlfriend or boyfriend to come to appointments.

5. What Side Effects Can These Medications Have?

Of all the medications Dr. Amen prescribes, he thinks that stimulants are the safest. He has never had to hospitalize a patient for a bad side effect and he has never had a side effect that did not go away once he stopped the medication.

Any medication can have side effects, including allergies to the medication (usually exhibited by a rash). Because each patient is different it is important to work together with your physician to find the best medication with the least amount of side effects. The following list may not include rare or unusual side effects. Talk to your doctor if you experience anything different since starting the medication.

Common Side Effects

These often go away after about 2-3 weeks, or if the dose of the medication is lowered. Rarely, as the medication wears off there may be a rebound effect where the hyperactivity or moodiness becomes worse than before the medication was started. Dosage adjustments usually help rebound.

lack of appetite: one of the most common side effects of these medications is a decreased appetite. Some ways to deal with this problem include: eat a good breakfast, add afternoon and evening snacks, take the medication after meals, rather than before. Some teens become hungry near bedtime. Unfortunately, some parents think that their hunger is no more than a manipulative ploy to stay up later and engage the teen in a battle. The medication really does affect appetite. If the teen is hungry later on and they did not have much to eat at dinner it is often a good idea to give them a late evening meal or snack. For some people a lack of appetite is a significant problem and the medication may need to be changed or adjusted. Some of Dr. Amen's patients use nutritional supplements, such as Ensure, to "ensure" they get enough calories and nutrients.

trouble falling asleep: some people experience insomnia. If they do, Dr. Amen either gives them a lower dose in the late afternoon or eliminates the last dose. In cases where there are problems when the last dose is eliminated, he may try giving a small dose of the stimulant right before bedtime. For insomnia, he often recommends a concoction of 6 ounces of warm milk with a tablespoon of vanilla and a tablespoon of sugar or honey. This seems to have a nice sedating effect for many people.

headaches or stomach aches: commonly, patients may complain of headaches or stomach aches. These typically go away after several weeks. Tylenol and ibuprofen (Advil) seem to be helpful for the headaches, taking the medication with food often decreases the stomach problems.

irritability, crankiness, crying, emotional sensitivity, staring into spaces, loss of interest in friends: some patients experience moodiness and minor personality changes. These side effects often go away in a week or two. If they don't, the medication often needs to be changed, maybe to an antidepressant.

Less Common Side Effects

tics: Some patients develop tics (such as eye blinking, throat clearing, head jerking) on the medication. If that happens it is important to discuss it with your doctor. Sometimes the tics go away on their own, sometimes higher doses of the medication may improve the tics and sometimes the medication has to be stopped. If the stimulant is very helpful, doctors might add another medication (such as clonidine or haloperidol) along with the stimulant to help with the tics. A complicating factor with tics, is that a high percentage of patients with tic disorders, such as Gilles de la Tourette's Syndrome (manifested by having both motor and vocal tics) have ADD. Sometimes it is hard to know if the medication caused the tics or were the tics already present, but worsened by the medication.

growth slowing: there use to be a concern about stimulants stunting growth, but the long term studies show that even though it may slow growth for a period of about a year, in the long run children usually catch up to where they should be.

rapid pulse or increased blood pressure: if a patient notices chest pain or a heart flutter it is important to notify the physician.

nervous habits: picking at the skin, stuttering and hair pulling can sometimes occur with these medications.

**The side effects of having untreated
ADD are immeasurably worse than
those caused by the medication!**

6. What Could Happen If This Medication Is Stopped Suddenly?

There are no medical problems to stopping the medication suddenly. A few people may experience irritability, moodiness, trouble sleeping or increased hyperactivity for a few days if they have been on daily medication for a long time. Often, it is better to stop the medication gradually over time (a week or so).

7. How Long Will The Medication Be Needed?

There is no way to know how long a person may need to take the medication. The patient, doctor, parent, teacher and spouse need to work together to find out what is right for each person. Sometimes the medication is only needed for a few years, sometimes it is needed for many years. Medication is an essential component of treatment for ADD and a person outgrows it or finds an alternative therapy that works (such as brainwave biofeedback), they need to remain on the medication. Without proper treatment, ADD is a serious disorder!

8. Does This Medication Interact With Other Medications?

It is a good idea to check with your doctor before mixing any prescription medications.

When stimulants are used with tricyclic antidepressants they may cause confusion, irritability, hallucinations or emotional outbursts. Sometimes, however, combining stimulants with antidepressants can be a powerfully positive combination (everyone is different). It is not a good idea to combine stimulants with nasal decongestants (such as medications that contain pseudoephedrine or related medications), because rapid pulse or high blood pressure may develop. If nasal decongestion is severe, it is better to use a nasal spray.

Many patients with ADD, may become cranky or more hyperactive on antihistamines (such as Benadryl). If medicine for allergies is needed, ask for one of the antihistamines that does not enter the brain (such as Hismanal).

Check with the pharmacist before giving any over-the-counter medication.

9. Does This Medication Stop Working At Puberty?

No! For most people it continues to work into adulthood. If it does lose its effectiveness, the dose may need to be increased or switching to another stimulant may be helpful. For the vast majority of people with ADD, it does not stop working at puberty (which many physicians used to tell parents).

10. Why Does This Medication Require A Special Prescription?

Prescriptions for Ritalin, Dexedrine and Desoxyn are written on special prescriptions known as "triplicates" (Cylert is written on a regular prescription). They must be filled within 7 days of the time the prescription is dated. Ritalin, Dexedrine and Desoxyn are controlled medications because some adults have been known to abuse them. This is rare in the doses prescribed for ADD. In fact, the research shows that children who are adequately treated for ADD have a much lower percentage of drug abuse as teenagers and adults than those kids with ADD who were never treated with medication. This medication does not cause illegal drug use or addiction!

11. What If My Child Or I Have Problems Remembering To Take The Medication?

Remembering to take medication 3-5 times a day can be difficult, even for people who do not have ADD. Forgetfulness is a common symptom of ADD and when the medication has worn off, the person is fully ADD again. If forgetfulness is a chronic problem, don't blame or be upset. Look for solutions. Here are two solutions: try switching to a slow release form of the medication; or get an alarm system (such as an electronic watch with 5 alarms) to help you re-member.

12. What About The Negative News Media Reports On These Medications?

It is critical to get your medical information from your doctor. Not from talk show hosts or the local news program. Many people have erroneous ideas about stimulant medication. If you hear things that worry you, check with your doctor before making any decisions.

** When you have questions, please write them down so that you can talk about them at your next appointment. If you are ever worried or concerned about a side effect please do not hesitate to call your doctor! He or she would rather know sooner than later.

Chapter 21:

A.D.D. and Your Legal Rights

We feel it is very important for teens with ADD to understand that there are legal protections for people with disabilities. Even though you do not want to think of yourself as having a disability there may be times when you may need help or protection. There are basic protections provided to people with disabilities in the United States. The following is a summary of several pertinent laws and statutes. Do not take this as legal advice, but as a guideline to seek appropriate help when necessary.

The 5th and 14th Amendments of the Constitution

The 5th and 14th amendments of the Constitution provide for due process and equal protection of all citizens under the law. This includes protection for people with disabilities.

Individuals with Disabilities Act (IDEA)

The Individuals With Disabilities Act mandates that public school districts which receive federal funds must provide a "free appropriate public education" to children and teens with disabilities.

Public Law 94-142

Public Law 94-142, which is also known as the Education for all Handicapped Children Act of 1975, is the federal law that states that every handicapped child and teen has the right to a free and appropriate public education in the least restrictive environment. This law also provides that each handicapped child and teen:

-- is guaranteed a culturally unbiased, valid assessment of his or her needs,

-- is to have an individualized education program designed to meet his or her unique needs,

-- is guaranteed specific procedures to insure his or her rights and those of parents (due process procedures).

The law says that all handicapped individuals need and have the right to an education in order to become self-sufficient and as productive as possible in adult society. Also, the handicapped children should be educated as much as possible with regular students (in the least restrictive environment).

The Rehabilitation Act of 1973 (RA)

The Rehabilitation Act of 1973 essentially outlaws discrimination against individuals with disabilities in education, employment (including federal government employment) and access to the benefits of federal programs by federal agencies and federal grant and contract recipients. Section 504 of this act defines the term disability.

The American With Disabilities Act (ADA)

The American With Disabilities Act outlaws discrimination against individuals with disabilities in private sector employment and state and local government activities and programs. It extends protection of the Rehabilitation Act of 1973 to individuals with disabilities who are employed by the Congress. Unlike the Rehabilitation Act of 1973, the ADA's protections do not depend on the receipt of federal funds.

In order to obtain the protections of the RA and ADA, it is necessary to establish that you: 1) are an "individual with a disability"; and 2) are "otherwise qualified"; and 3) were denied a job, education, or other benefit "solely by reason" of the disability; and 4) the individual, firm, or governmental agency which refused you is covered by the RA or ADA.

Under both the RA and ADA, an "individual with a disability" is any individual who:

 (i) has a physical or mental impairment which substantially limits one or more of such person's major life activities,

(ii) has a record of such an impairment, or

(iii) is regarded as having such an impairment.

The second and third definitions are intended to protect individuals who previously had a disability but do not now, and those people who are treated as though they had a disability but do not.

The definition of a "physical or mental impairment" includes: "any mental or psychological disorder, such as mental retardation, organic brain syndrome, emotional or mental illness, and specific learning disabilities." Even though ADD is not specifically mentioned in the regulations, it is recognized as a "mental or psychological disorder." The effects of medication are not to be considered in assessing whether an individual has an "impairment." The severity of one's ADD or LD must meet these statutes without considering the potential benefits of medications.

The RA and ADA clearly apply to individuals with ADD and LD as long as these disorders substantially limit a major life activity, such as learning or job performance.

U. S. Education Department

On September 16, 1991 the U.S. Education Department issued a memorandum recognizing children with ADD as eligible for special education and related services under federal law. The policy makes clear that children with ADD qualify for special education and related services solely on the basis of ADD, when the ADD itself impairs educational performance or learning, under both (i) Public Law 94-142, Individuals with Disabilities Act (IDEA) statutes and regulations; and (ii) Section 504 of the 1973 Rehabilitation Act plus its implementing regulations. Schools are required to evaluate students suspected of having ADD and afford their families due process hearings in case there are disagreements over such evaluations. In addition, schools are required to have special education programs and services specifically designed for ADD education needs. It also requires regular classroom adaptations for children and teens who do not need special education assistance.

Job Accommodations For ADD

Reasonable accommodations are required for workers who qualify under these statutes. Accommodations are of three general types:

1) those required to ensure equal opportunity in the job application process,

2) those which enable the individual with a disability to perform the essential features of a job, and

3) those which enable individuals with disabilities to enjoy the same benefits and privileges as those available to individuals without disabilities.

Reasonable accommodations for ADD and LD often include the following:

• part-time or modified work schedules
• providing or modifying equipment or devices
• job restructuring
• reassignment to a vacant position
• adjusting/modifying examinations, training materials, or policies
• providing readers or interpreters, and
• making the workplace accessible to and usable by people with disabilities

Despite the fears of employers, the accommodations actually required for individuals with ADD or LD are generally not expensive or extensive. The President's Committee on Employment for People with Disabilities has concluded that:

-- 31% of accommodations cost nothing
-- 50% cost less than $50
-- 69% cost less then $500
-- 88% cost less than $1,000

Certainly, in many cases, job retraining costs much more than the accommodations necessary to keep a valued employee.

Specific Sample Work Accommodations for People With ADD/LD

** Employees with ADD need structure. ADD adults are often successful in the military because there is a high level of structure provided.

** Pressure often disorganizes the ADD employee. Give them enough time to do their job, without undue pressure.

** Use praise more than threats. Threats and anger trigger off negative memories in the past for most ADD people. An employer is likely to get much more productivity from the ADD employee by using praise and encouragement.

** Help with organization. ADD employees often have serious problems with organization. Teaching them effective ways to organize their work area and time may help them significantly.

** Give simple instructions and have the employee repeat them back. As I've mentioned, people with ADD may only process 30%

of what is said. It is critical to check with them to ensure they understand what is expected of them.

** Modify hiring tests and on-the-job performance tests. People with ADD often need more time to complete tests to show what they really know. Employers could lose a valuable asset by excluding someone based on timed tests. In a similar way, on-the-job performance tests need to be modified so that the ADD person is not at a disadvantage.

** Supplement verbal instructions with visual instructions.

** Adjust work schedules when possible. Many people with ADD have trouble getting up early in the morning and do better with work schedules which begin later in the day. Also, provide a grace period for tardiness and have the employee, when late, be able to make up time at the end of the day (as long as this won't interfere with the behavior or morale of other employees).

Other suggestions from Carol Means, Ed.D of the Job Accommodations Network at West Virginia University include:

Computer related:

word processing programs with spell checkers and grammar checkers;

software organizers, such as those by Borland, Micro Logic and Micro Systems

software flow charts

computer screen reading systems/reading machines

Clerical:

color coding
color templates
electronic and desktop organizers,
        such as those by Casio, Franklin and Sharp
cassette recorders
telephone recorders/adapter switches
dictaphones
audio prompts/cue cards
electronic spelling masters

Memory aids:

personal assistant devices
timers, counters
Neuropage

Time management skills:

goal setting
staying on one task until it is finished

Managing the physical environment:

mapping

room enclosures
tinnitus maskers/environmental sound machines

For more information contact the Job Accommodation Network's toll free number at (800) 526-7234 or (800) ADA-WORK. Person's calling from Canada may call (800) 526-2262.

Chapter 22:

A.D.D. and Your Future

Here are the main points to remember:

-- ADD is a biological condition
-- it is usually inherited
-- it is not your fault
-- without treatment serious problems may follow you
   (at home, school, work and in relationships)
-- education of the family and support system is often essential
-- medication is an important part of the treatment
-- dose of medication is highly individual
-- you may have to try several different medications before you
   find the right one
-- after diagnosis and treatment it's important to rethink some
   of the misconceptions you might have about yourself, such as
   "I'm lazy or not very smart."
-- stay away from all forms of illicit drugs, don't drink alcohol
   because it works to intensify ADD
-- become part of an ADD support group. Helping others is one
   of the best ways to help yourself.

ADD, for most people, is a life long condition. Continue with your
treatment. NEVER GIVE UP ON YOURSELF.

Glossary

AREAS OF THE BRAIN

cingulate gyrus--a system that runs down the top/center of the brain that allows us to shift attention or move from idea to idea. If the cingulate system is malfunctioning or overactive you can become stuck on thoughts (obsessions) and behaviors (compulsions). Other problems include worrying, holding onto hurts from the past, argumentativeness, and oppositional behavior. Some other disorders that involve this brain system are obsessive-compulsive disorder, eating disorders and chronic pain.

limbic system--a more primitive system located at the very center of the brain that sets the emotional tone of the mind. The limbic system also controls appetite and sleep cycles, promotes bonding and modulates motivation. If the limbic system is overactive or malfunctions there are problems with moodiness, irritability, depression, increased negative thinking, appetite and sleep problems, social isolation and decreased motivation.

pre-frontal cortex--the most evolved system of the brain located just behind the forehead. This area is involved with maintaining focus, attention span, judgment, impulse control, critical thinking and creating conscious thought. If the pre-frontal cortex is not functioning properly a person may experience problems with distractibility, impulsivity, procrastination, short attention span, misperceptions, poor judgment, social and/or test anxiety or unavailability of emotions.

temporal lobes--area of the brain located on either side of the brain underneath the temples. They store our experiences and help us define our sense of ourselves. When the temporal lobes function normally, we have a clear sense of who we are, our life situations and the nature of things around us. Abnormal activity in the temporal lobes can cause abnormal percepetions, periods of spaciness or confusion and rage outbursts.

MEDICATION

anti-obsessive-antidepressants--includes Prozac, Paxil, Zoloft, Anafranil, Luvox and Effexor. These medications increase the neurotransmitter serotonin in the brain.

anti-seizure medication--(also refered to as anticonvulsants) includes Tegretol, Neurontin and Depakote. These medications are often helpful for ADD people that have violent outbursts. These medications can particulary help those people with temporal lobe dysfunction.

stimulant medications--includes Ritalin, Dexedrine, Desoxyn, Adderall and Cylert. This class of medication helps the underactive parts of your brain become more accessible to you.

STREET DRUGS

amphetamines (street stimulants)--drugs such as methamphetamine and cocaine. These drugs are very strong stimulants, but can be **very** dangerous when used as a street drug since you can not control what other poisonous substances have been added.

Frequent, and even one time use, can have serious side effects. . . even death.

hallucinagens--mushrooms, acid, LSD, angel dust, etc. These are drugs that alter your perceptions. You may see, hear, taste, feel and even smell things that are not really there. Often people think that they can feel or see scary things on them and they can end up hurting or even killing themselves during a bad trip. These drugs can often cause "flash backs" up to 20 or 30 years after stopping the drug!

inhalents--Substances like gasoline, white out, paint thinner, lighter fluid and glue. These like the other drugs can be very addic-tive. They are also directly processed by the brain and can cause im-mediate and irreparable damage. Even though most people don't think about it, inhalents are very, very dangerous.

MISCELLANEOUS

ADD--stands for Attention Deficit Disorder. Unlike what most people who don't know much about ADD think, ADD is a physical disorder of the brain. ADD affects millions of men, women, boys and girls across the world. These people commonly have problems with attention difficulties, distractibility, impulsivity and restless-ness. Most people DO NOT grow out of ADD!

ADHD--the "classic" type of Attention Deficit Disorder which in-cludes hyperactivity as one of its chief symptoms.

ADD depressive subtype--the type of ADD where people tend to consistently have negative feelings and low energy. This usually

involves the limbic system and responds to antidepressant medications. This is different from clinical depression because the symptoms for ADD depressive subtype are seen in childhood and stay consistent over a long period of time.

ADD overfocused subtype--the type of ADD where people are unable to shift their attention easily from one subject to another. This involves problems with cingulate activity and usually responds to anti-obsessive-antidepressant medications

ADD violent/explosive subtype--the type of ADD where people can experience feelings ranging from panic or fear for no reason, irritability and rage outbursts to dark suicidal or homicidal thoughts. The temporal lobes are usually dyfunctioning with this type of ADD. Antiseizure medications such as Tegretol or Depakote can help people with this type of ADD.

neurotransmitters--includes serotonin, dopamine and norepinephrine. These are chemicals in the brain that help keep our brains active. Sometimes there is an imbalance of neurotransmitters in different parts of the brain, so we use medications to help bring these levels back to normal.

SPECT--Single Photon Emission Computed Tomography. This type of brain study allows doctors to look at how our brains work.